# Medea • Hippolytus • Helen

Euripides' dramas center on great human beings who find the cause of tragedy within themselves and fight the demon of their own souls:

**Medea**—a passionate woman, her love turns into bitter hatred when betrayed by her ambitious husband . . .

**Hippolytus**—a chaste youth, he spurns illicit love and suffers the wrath of a king . . .

**Helen**—victim of a rivalry between the gods, she remains faithful to her husband, despite danger, temptation and the threat of death.

As Rex Warner points out in his illuminating introduction to his brilliant translations of these great plays, *"It is in showing the individuality and also the universality of suffering that Euripides deserves the title of 'the most tragic poet.' . . . We shall admire him not only for brilliance but for understanding, the understanding of heart and mind, unbiased, unprejudiced, but in its nature full of sympathy, looking for good and very sensitive to pity where good is not to be found . . . [his] productions are as near to timeless as are any that are known to us."*

# THREE GREAT PLAYS OF EURIPIDES

## MEDEA • HIPPOLYTUS • HELEN

*Translated by*
**Rex Warner**

A MERIDIAN BOOK

MERIDIAN
Published by the Penguin Group
Penguin Books USA Inc., 375 Hudson Street,
New York, New York 10014, U.S.A.
Penguin Books Ltd, 27 Wrights Lane,
London W8 5TZ, England
Penguin Books Australia Ltd, Ringwood,
Victoria, Australia
Penguin Books Canada Ltd, 10 Alcorn Avenue,
Toronto, Ontario, Canada M4V 3B2
Penguin Books (N.Z.) Ltd, 182–190 Wairau Road,
Auckland 10, New Zealand

Penguin Books Ltd, Registered Offices:
Harmondsworth, Middlesex, England

Published by Meridian, an imprint of Dutton Signet, a division of Penguin
Books USA Inc. This is an authorized reprint of a hardcover edition published by
The Bodley Head Limited. For information address The Bodley Head Limited,
10 Earlham Street, London WC 2.

First Meridian Printing, © October, 1994
10   9   8   7   6

Introduction © 1958 by Rex Warner

*Medea*, first published 1944; *Hippolytus*, first published 1950; *Helen*, first published 1951.

Previously published in a Meridian Classic edition and in a Mentor edition.

 REGISTERED TRADEMARK–MARCA REGISTRADA

LIBRARY OF CONGRESS CATALOG CARD NUMBER: 83-50743

Printed in the United States of America

# Contents

# Introduction: Euripides and His Age

ONE OF THE delights—one might say too, one of the advantages—of the study of ancient Greek history is that things seem to happen very clearly and distinctly. They happen also very rapidly, so that we get the impression that in the course of a mere century or so, there have been more events and more changes than we shall find in much longer periods taken from the histories of other countries.

And in all Greek history it would be difficult to find so rich, varied and momentous a period as that covered by the life of the Athenian dramatist Euripides. He was born probably in 485 B.C. and died abroad, probably in 406. Five years before his birth the battle of Marathon was fought, a victory for the new free Athenian democracy over what were represented as the hordes of Easterners, races who, in the modern Athenian sense, were 'without the law.' And when Euripides was a child of five he may have watched from his father's estate on the island of Salamis the great naval battle which finally shattered the hopes of Persian monarchs to extend their conquests westward, and which marked Athens out not only as a new political organisation but as the greatest sea power in the Mediterranean.

The child was no doubt too young to experience fully the glory of those early days of Athenian innovation, prestige and sudden greatness. Here he differed from the other two great dramatists of the century; for Aeschylus had fought at Marathon and Sophocles, as a youth, led the choir that sang the hymn of victory after Salamis. Yet still the days of the youth and early manhood of Euripides were passed in what most Athenians would have regarded as a blaze of patriotic splendour. We, looking back at those times, can see them as a unique period in the history of the world, a period in which were laid the foundations of our present-day civilisation. These years saw the invention of drama, the fine flowering of sculpture and of architecture, the foundations laid of law and politics, of science and philosophy. But all these were merely aspects of a way of life achieved miraculously, it seems to us who look back on it all, by a few generations of men. In ways unparalleled before in history men sought to understand, to explain and, at least in so far as human relationships were concerned, to reshape the world in which they lived. They looked at everything in heaven and earth with strangely unprejudiced eyes, and from what they saw they made new products of theory, imagination and behaviour.

Many different individuals could be described as in their own ways representative of these tremendous years of the fifth century B.C. One can speak meaningfully of 'the age of Sophocles,' 'the age of Pericles,' or attribute 'ages' to Thucydides, Socrates and many others as well. But in thinking of 'the age of Euripides' one is, I believe, thinking of an age which, while being representatve of many important aspects of the fifth century, is also an age peculiarly close to that one in which we live today, and in reading Euripides himself we are without question reading the most 'modern' dramatist of the ancient world.

The two obvious characteristics of 'the age of Euripides' and of the 'modernity' of Euripides are, first, a most thoroughgoing kind of rationalism and, secondly, an emphasis on the individual (in particular on individual suffering) which had previously been unknown in the world's history. It does not surprise us to find that Socrates was a great admirer of Euripides' plays or that Aristotle called him 'the most tragic of the poets'—so long as by 'most tragic' we understand something like 'the poet most apt to feel and excite pity.'

Now the rationalism of the age of Euripides requires some explanation from an historical point of view. It is a rationalism that is both like and unlike our own brand, but in the days of Euripides it was, like so much else, an innovation. It is strongly criticised as such by the comic poet Aristophanes who groups Euripides and Socrates together as crack-brained theorists, likely by their doctrines to have a dangerous and disruptive influence on morality. And when we remember that Socrates, the saint and apostle of this kind of rationalism, was actually put to death by his own fellow-citizens for exercising a subversive influence, we can see that the new thought was not only a subject for comedy, but regarded by many respectable people as a real danger. Yet the Athenians, of all people, prided themselves on their deserved reputation as innovators and on the quite extraodinary freedom of speech which they enjoyed. No author in wartime has ever since been allowed to attack, from a public stage, the policies and personalities of his own government as Aristophanes did. Yet Socrates, a theorist not a politician, was put to death, and Euripides, with his reputation for this particular 'cleverness' was, in spite of his great popularity in some circles, suspected and disliked by the majority of the men in the street.

The future, as we can see now, was with Socrates and with Euripides. The plays of Euripides, after the poet's death, soon became much more popular than those of the two other great dramatists who, in his lifetime, had enjoyed much more success than he. The new comedy which replaced the old unique comedy of Aristophanes and which was in many respects comparable with the great plays we see today, derived much from the method of Euripides. While it is difficult to find in later European drama characters or plots which remind us of those of Aeschylus or of Sophocles, Euripides appears often as an originator or an inspirer. This, however, is perhaps rather the result of his 'individualism' than of his rationalism. And in discussing both of these qualities one must be careful not to suggest that 'modernity' is necessarily a merit. With regard to the new rationalism, in particular, one must admit that some of the criticisms of Aristophanes were valid.

The fact is that this rationalism was disruptive of

much that had been proved good. The men who fought at Marathon believed, some of them, in the new democracy, and all of them, we may be sure, were prepared to fight and die, as so many Greeks have done since then, for a peculiar and most vividly realised independence. But they believed too in the gods, in tradition, in notions of right and wrong that were accepted and taught rather than invented or discussed. They may well have been proud of the new ideas, the new techniques, the new modes of thought and expression for which their city was becoming famous; but they would have been, and some of them in their old age became, horrified at the fact that this new thought, once given scope, was no respecter of anything, whether person, institution, convention or idea that could not 'give an account of itself.' The gods themselves seemed to come under attack, and to the average sincere and unreflecting worshipper it would have been impossible to explain that these attacks were often a form of piety.

Two impulses, one worthy, one not so much so, worked together in the creation of Greek, and European, rationalism. There was the spirit which today we describe as 'scientific,' an unresting curiosity and a rigid respect for what, within the rules of thought, is 'truth'; and there was a form of applied science, in this case the application of intellect to the practical aim of securing power. These two impulses were often combined in the same persons. Professors (the 'sophists') existed who not only showed the keenest interest in 'truth' as we understand it, but also quite openly boasted that they could teach their pupils how, by persuasive argument, to make the untrue appear to be true and so win success in the law courts and in politics. Their brilliant and novel techniques of argument and discovery rested, usually, on a general scepticism. Gorgias of Leontini, for instance, a sophist who was very popular in Athens, had written a treatise in which he maintained (1) that nothing exists (2) that if anything does exist, it cannot be known, and (3) that, if it can be known, the knowledge cannot be communicated by language. Another famous sophist, Protagoras, declared that of the gods it was impossible to say either that they did or that they did not exist. He is credited with the statement 'Man is the measure,' a statement which, while it has many practical advantages, must appear to those who believe in God or the gods as dangerous and incomplete.

It seems that there is a sense in which thoroughgoing scepticism is of the greatest value, as it was in the different cases of Socrates and of Descartes; but for it to be valuable it must be, as it were, aimed at truth. One may admit ignorance without denying the possibility of knowledge. But once all knowledge becomes regarded as a mere convention, things become dangerous. We are close to the problem of *The Brothers Karamazov*, the problem as to whether or not 'All things are lawful.' In particular we are up against the problem of power. Has anyone any 'right' to resist the stronger, when resistance is likely to be ineffective? Has the stronger any 'duty' other than that of self-preservation? The problem is constantly present in fifth century literature. It is stated in perhaps the most precise form by Thucydides in his *Melian Dialogue,* but it is always recurring in Euripides and in the arguments attributed to Socrates.

Now it is undeniable that the new techniques of rationalism played a great part in bringing about conditions in which could exist such states of total moral chaos as that which Thucydides describes as existing after the revolution in Corcyra or after the plague in Athens. A rigid and not very intelligent conservative could easily maintain that it was from the new learning, from the sophists, from Euripides or Socrates, that arguments to justify political treachery, disrespect for the old, immorality in wives, disbelief in the gods and all the other vices of an age that had lost the simple uncritical purity of the past were derived. Such a critic would not observe that, while it was perfectly true that the new rationalism could equip anyone with apparently logical arguments on any subject, its leading practitioners were, in fact, devoted to truth and to humanity with an extraordinary fervour.

We observe also, both in Socrates and in Euripides, a kind of modesty, a quality rather rare among self-confessed rationalists past or present. Certainly they would have maintained that everything under the sun should be scrutinised, that nothing was in its nature immune from criticism and examination; but they were constantly aware that they were in the dark on a number of subjects. In this connexion it may be useful to refer briefly to Euripides' treatment of the gods. Here, it would seem, both in ancient and modern times, he has been both applauded and attacked for the wrong reasons.

Naïve atheists at all times have often claimed Euripides as one of their number. The claim is quite unjustified. It rests, presumably, on the fact that in many of his plays Euripides not only makes the gods behave badly, but also states clearly that they are behaving badly. It is therefore assumed that he cannot have believed in the existence of such beings. And sometimes an even more unwarrantable conclusion is drawn, namely, that he did not believe in any kind of divinity at all.

Now in the first place it should be remembered that all Greek tragedies were produced at a religious festival and that, with very few exceptions, they all dealt with stories taken from mythology about the doings of gods, heroes and great men of a distant past. In many of these stories the gods (there is no denying the fact) play a disreputable part. Euripides was not the first dramatist to have observed this. Aeschylus is at least as deeply moved as Euripides by the problem of reconciling mythology with any reasonable or lofty idea of divinity. He is profoundly religious in his outlook and (an important point to note) often religious in a way that is by no means familiar to us. In his treatment of the story of Prometheus, for example, he shows us in the one play out of three which survives a Zeus behaving in the most arbitrary, cruel and tyrannical manner. Prometheus may indeed be overproud, but he remains the 'hero' of the play. Yet by the end of the trilogy the tension has been resolved. Some sort of reconcilement (we do not know exactly what) has taken place between Zeus and Prometheus. But for such a reconcilement to have taken place at all each must have made some concession to the other. Therefore the omnipotent ruler of gods and men, Zeus, must have admitted that he made a mistake. The gods themselves, in other words, must be capable of evolving, like men have evolved, from a kind of savagery to a higher way of life. Such an idea must be completely foreign to those who use the word 'god' in the context of Jewish or Christian tradition. And indeed it is nearly always a mistake, though an unavoidable one, to translate the Greek word 'theos' by our word 'god.' Often the word means nothing more than a 'force,' whether psychological or material. Physical love, for instance, is a 'force' of this sort and, as is shown in the *Hippolytus* can be, although a 'theos,' both destructive and, by normal standards, immoral. The sun also is a 'theos,' and Anaxagoras, the philosopher, was accused before the courts of impiety when he maintained that it was a red-hot stone. These 'forces and these impressive distant objects, like the sun or the stars, undoubtedly existed and undoubtedly had to be reckoned with. Yet to a moralist they must appear often unjust and irresponsible, and to an intellectual they must sometimes seem absurd. Later philosophers, Plato and Aristotle, seem to have worked in the direction of some kind of monotheism. Such a doctrine is at least intellectually respectable. And Plato, as a moralist, would certainly have expurgated the old stories of the gods before they were allowed in the hands of the young.

Euripides also is in his own way a moralist and he feels the moralist's dilemma when he thinks of the gods and of the extreme difficulty of justifying their ways to men. The servant in *Hippolytus,* appealing to the goddess Aphrodite, says, reasonably enough, we think: 'Gods should be wiser and more moderate than men.' Yet the audience have already heard from this particular goddess that she has planned the most savage action against innocent people simply out of motives of wounded vanity. She is, from our human point of view, definitely not 'wiser and more moderate than men.' On the showing of the play any father of the church could easily pronounce Aphrodite to be a demon rather than a 'true god.' But the Athenian audience do not seem to have found this play impious. It was one of the few of Euripides' plays which received first prize, and Euripides himself, in pointing out that in the divine order there are contrary and opposing forces, seems to be merely stating a fact of nature. Still it is undoubtedly a fact of nature which he finds incongruous and unpleasant. The god-fearing Hippolytus himself is allowed to say: 'I wish the race of men had power to curse the gods.' And in one of the choruses, expressing, we may reasonably guess, the author's point of view, we read the conflicting statements:

> Greatly indeed it will ease me of grief, when it
>   comes to my mind,
> The thought of the gods.
> Yet, though guessing in hope at their wisdom,
> I am downcast when I look at the fortunes and
>   actions of mortals.

Indeed 'guessing in hope' is a fair enough description of Euripides' rationalistic approach to the subject. He is far from saying that the gods can be ignored and even further from maintaining that they do not exist. But their interventions or noninterventions certainly puzzle him. We shall find nowhere in his plays an attempt to show, as Aeschylus does in the *Oresteia*, the working out of a divine purpose which, though difficult indeed to discern, can still be reverently acknowledged. In the *Medea*, as in several other plays, the gods seem to play no important part at all, except to provide an escape route at the end. In the *Hippolytus* the gods are undoubtedly important, though, as always in Euripides, it is, dramatically, the men and women who chiefly matter. In this play there is a touching beauty in the young man's worship of the virgin goddess Artemis, and there is something terrifying, even horrible, about the ruthless and immense power of Aphrodite. Most certainly, any audience must feel, such a power 'exists' and must be reckoned with. The same lesson can be drawn from the *Bacchae*, the great work of Euripides' old age. In the *Helen* again the emphasis is on the fortunes, the romantic sufferings and escapes of men rather than on the gods. It is in the background to the story that the part of the gods is played, and the part they play is, quite simply, that of deceivers. Because of jealousy among the gods, all the sufferings of the Trojan war are allowed to take place in a cause that was entirely meaningless, since the main object of the expedition was never at Troy at all.

We may conclude then that, while on most subjects Euripides as a rationalist is easily intelligible to us to-day, since he speaks the same logical language, with regard to the gods he is not so easy to understand. It would be wrong to call him an atheist or an agnostic or, in our sense, a 'believer.'

But when we consider his attitude towards men and women—what I have called his individualism—we shall find him almost invariably modern in our own sense of the word. This fact may be partly explained by some similarities between his experience and ours. As we have seen he lived in an age of startling discovery and invention and, in particular, an age of questioning during which all established notions of thought and behaviour came in for examination and criticism. He also lived in an age of almost continuous warfare. Most of his plays were produced during the years of the long struggle between Athens and Sparta, and it would appear that Euripides, more than any other writer of antiquity, was moved by the horrors and wastages of war and by the sufferings of its victims. Yet this concern for the sufferings of individuals goes much beyond mere pacifism. War may produce numerically the most spectacular examples of human suffering, and in wartime, as Thucydides pointed out, with the collapse of normal restraint man's nature reveals a peculiar savagery. Yet if there were no wars there would still be suffering. Moreover a slave, a woman, an ordinary man can suffer as much as a king. It is in showing the individuality and also the universality of suffering that Euripides deserves the title of 'the most tragic poet.'

Here also, though he had his ardent admirers, he offended the convention of his times. Sometimes offence was caused merely to the theatrical convention. It was assumed proper, for instance, that all kings on the stage should at least be well dressed. Many complaints are heard of the effrontery of Euripides in bringing on, in the *Helen,* no less a king than Menelaus dressed in rags and appearing indistinguishable from a common mortal who has been shipwrecked. Much more serious conventions were offended by Euripides' treatment of women, and here in particular the names of Medea and of Phaedra are mentioned. Both are represented as women in love (though the love of Medea has turned to hatred) and the representation was certainly considered by many critics improper. It was not that the Athenians objected to the presentation on the stage of women with powerful, pathetic or even vicious characters. The Clytemnestra of Aeschylus and many other women in other plays are there to prove the fact. What really caused offence, it seems, was the naturalism of Euripides' method. His critics would accuse him of lack of dignity and would object that it was both bad art and bad morals to show on the stage a queen who was not only in love, but was in the grip of a guilty love and, worst of all, seemed to express this love in language that was very like that of an ordinary Athenian woman, except that it was remarkably acute language, throwing light on dark places in the soul and often on places which the man in the street preferred to believe did not exist. His admirers, on the other hand, amongst whom we can confidently imagine Socrates, admired him not only for what was fashionable (the skill and variety of verbal argument, e.g. in the scenes between Jason and Medea) but also for his new and penetrating psychological insight. They could rightly maintain that whether Euripides' women were 'good' or 'bad' was not the point and they could give, in Helen or in Iphigeneia, examples of 'goodness' which could balance the 'badness' of Medea or Phaedra. But the important point was that the women were real and real in a new way because they had been created out of a new kind of sympathy. The stories were, as was necessary, the stories of mythology, but these mythical characters had, as it were, become reborn as contemporary human beings each of whom was an individual in his or her own right.

This intense interest of the dramatist in the individual has much to do with determining the method of his work. There is a sense in which it may be said that Euripides, out of courtesy to the dramatic convention of the day, gives his plays a prologue and an epilogue, in which very often divine beings are the speakers, and between the two writes the real play which is concerned solely with human beings. But such a view is an over-simplification. In some plays (the *Bacchae* in particular) the gods are very much part of the action. And many of the prologues (those of the *Medea* and *Helen*, for instance) are spoken by human actors and spoken perfectly in character. The prologues, however, unlike the plots of the plays, do seem to conform to a general rule. Their purpose is quickly to put before the audience a statement of what the play will be about and sometimes how it will end. This was necessary dramatically since, though the Athenian audience would certainly be acquainted with the stories on which the plays were usually based, Euripides was very apt to use new stories altogether or put in characteristic variations of his own in the stories known already. As for the epilogues, Euripides has often been blamed here for a kind of carelessness and indifference, for using the *deus ex machina* merely as a useful way of either getting out of some of the difficulties of the plot or else of satisfying religious convention although the real play is already over. These criticisms are certainly not justified if applied to the three plays included in this volume. The *Medea* ends finely and naturally, the element of the miraculous merely intensifying the human emotion which we have felt throughout the drama. In the *Hippolytus* (perhaps the most perfectly constructed of all Euripides' plays), the appearance at the end of the goddess Artemis is strangely moving and so too is her withdrawal as she leaves the stage finally to the dying son and the father with whom he becomes reconciled. In the *Helen* one may possibly find something ridiculous in the sudden appearance at the end of the Dioscuri who have done nothing whatever to help their sister during all the long time that she needed help. But this play is more of a comedy than a tragedy. The ending is neat and, if slightly funny, not, I think, inappropriate.

So far as the structure of the central part of the play is concerned, Euripides follows the tragic convention, though introducing some variations of his own. In general the structure is one of 'episodes' or acts, each separated from each by a choral ode. The plays lead up to or contain some violent action, and this violent action invariably takes place off the stage. It is then reported by means of the traditional Messenger's speech. Euripides is justly famous for his messengers' speeches and there are no finer examples of these in all his work than are to be found in the *Medea* and in the *Hippolytus*. As for the 'episodes,' the dialogue between actors, he was much admired for his 'recognition scenes' (such as the one in the *Helen*) and he was both admired and criticised for his expression of emotion in passages between the actors written in lyric metres and accompanied by music. His use of the chorus is very different from that of Aeschylus and considerably different from that of Sophocles. In Aeschylus the chorus often plays a large part in the play. It is closely associated with the actors, and indeed in the *Prometheus* it shares in the fate of the hero. But in Euripides, as we have seen, the real drama is confined to the men and women taking part in it. The chorus perform the role of sympathetic listeners and commentators, or, on the occasions of their formal odes, provide the audience with a kind of musical and poetic relief from the difficulties or horrors of the action. A good example of this last function of the chorus is to be found in the famous ode in the *Hippolytus*, sung at the moment when Phaedra leaves the stage to commit suicide. It has nothing whatever to do with the action of the play; indeed it deliberately takes us out of this action into an ideal world where such happenings are assumed to be impossible and then gradually brings us back again, in a strangely different frame of mind, to contemplate the tragedy that has, in fact, taken place. In modern productions of

Greek plays the chorus notoriously presents more difficulties than anything else to the producer, and a producer may well be tempted to dispense with it altogether if, as in Euripides, it plays so small a part in the action. Yet if we do leave out the chorus from any one of Euripides' plays, a loss is immediately apparent. The chorus, active or inactive, is an integral part of the drama and must remain to fascinate or to plague producers.

And what we have said of the chorus may be said also of other elements in the plays or in the mind of Euripides which, for the sake of convenience, we have attempted to isolate but which in fact are all parts of a living unity. I have emphasized in particular what I have called the rationalism and the individualism, or humanity, of Euripides; but there is no conflict between these two and each is interpenetrated by the other. Other qualities also deserve emphasis; for example it could be maintained that Euripides is the first 'romantic' writer in European literature. Certainly one is attracted to him by different elements of his genius at different periods of one's own life. We too, like some of his admirers in ancient Athens, are sometimes immediately impressed by his 'cleverness' which we may find, according to our own natures, either fascinating or repulsive. But in the end we shall see that 'cleverness' is much too weak and shabby a word to use of this poet. We shall admire him not only for brilliance but for understanding, the understanding of heart and mind, unbiased, unprejudiced, but in its nature full of sympathy, looking for good and very sensitive to pity where good is not to be found. He is very much a person of a particular age in a particular city; but the chief glory of that age and that city is that its productions are as near to timeless as are any that are known to us.

—REX WARNER

# The MEDEA
## of
# EURIPIDES

# The Characters

MEDEA, *princess of Colchis and wife of*
JASON, *son of Aeson, king of Iolcos*
TWO CHILDREN *of Medea and Jason*
KREON, *king of Corinth*
AIGEUS, *king of Athens*
NURSE *to Medea*
TUTOR *to Medea's children*
MESSENGER
*and*
CHORUS OF CORINTHIAN WOMEN

# Introduction

THE ATHENIAN AUDIENCE who saw the first performance of Euripides' *Medea* at the state dramatic contest in 431 B.C. and who awarded the third prize to Euripides would have been familiar with the whole story of the chief characters, and we, twenty-three centuries later, are handicapped in our understanding of the play if we have not at least some knowledge of the same story.

The Athenians would have known Medea as a barbarian princess and as a sorceress, related to the gods. She came from the faraway land of Colchis at the eastern extremity of the Black Sea, where her father, King Aietes, a sorcerer himself and the son of Helios, god of the Sun, kept the Golden Fleece. Here Jason had come with the Argonauts, the first expedition of western Greeks against the eastern barbarians. Medea had fallen in love with him and by her aid he was able to avoid the traps laid for him by Aietes, to regain the Golden Fleece and to escape, taking Medea with him. She, to assist the escape, had murdered her own brother, strewing the pieces of his body over the water so that her father's fleet, while collecting the fragments for burial, might lose time in the pursuit of the fugitives.

Medea and Jason then settled in Jason's hereditary kingdom of Iolcos, where Pelias, his uncle, still cheated him of his rights. Medea, hoping to do Jason a favour, persuaded the daughters of Pelias to attempt, under her guidance, a magic rejuvenation of their father. The old man was to be killed, cut in pieces and then, with the aid of herbs and incantations, restored to his first youth. The unsuspecting daughters did as they were told and Medea left them with their father's blood upon their hands. However, the result of this crime was no advancement for Jason but rather exile for him, Medea and their two children.

From Iolcos they came to Corinth, the scene of Euripides' play. Here Jason, either, as he says himself, wishing to strengthen his own economic position, or, as Medea thinks, because he was tired of his dangerous foreign wife, put her aside and married the daughter of Kreon, king of Corinth. It is at this point that the action of the play begins; but the Athenian audience would know well enough what the plot would be. They would know that Medea, in her jealous rage, would destroy both Kreon and his daughter by means of a poisoned robe which clung to the flesh and burned it; that, despairing of her children's safety and wishing through them to injure Jason in every way, she would kill them with her own hands; and that finally, by supernatural means, she would escape to their own city and take refuge with the old king Aigeus.

It is always an enjoyable exercise to translate one language into another; but the translator's own pleasure in his task does not in itself justify him in submitting the results of his effort to the public. And as this play, the *Medea*, has already been translated several times into English, and, in the version of Professor Gilbert Murray, has enjoyed considerable success on the stage, it may well be asked why yet another version should be produced.

It may be said, in general, that, Greek and Latin literature being so rich, the more translations there are the better. None of them will, in the nature of things, convey the full force of the original, but each may succeed in revealing a different aspect. So new translations do not so much supersede as complement old ones. Yet without doubt some translations are better than others and, if the purpose of a translation is to convey something of the spirit of the original to those who are ignorant of the original language, then I think that the laborious transliterators are more to be commended than the brilliant distortionists. For these seem to be the two methods of work, one of which must be chosen.

When we read:

> He came and, standing in the midst, explained
> The peace rejected, but the truce obtained

we know that we are reading Pope and not Homer. Yet Pope is himself a great poet, so that we admire his work, however different may be the whole of its atmosphere from that in which the Achilles and Hector of Homer lived. Pope and Dryden are the most brilliant of all the distortionists.

But when the translator is not a great poet and still distorts, then there is much less to recommend him. Under these circumstances it seems far safer to stick as closely as possible to the original. Indeed even those who are poets themselves have rightly adopted this method. Browning, for instance, translates almost word for word and, to my mind, is the more admirable for that, in spite of his rigidities and obscurities.

So in the following translation I have attempted rather to follow his example than that of the more ambitious versifiers. In some respects I have gone even further; for no rhyme is used either for the dialogue or for the choruses, and by employing a longer line than the line of English blank verse I have been able to avoid the compression that is inevitable if the commoner metre is used.

# The MEDEA of EURIPIDES

*[In front of Medea's house in Corinth.
Enter from the house Medea's nurse.]*

NURSE

How I wish the Argo never had reached the land
Of Colchis, skimming through the blue Symplegades,
Nor ever had fallen in the glades of Pelion
The smitten fir-tree to furnish oars for the hands
Of heroes who in Pelias's name attempted
The Golden Fleece! For then my mistress Medea
Would not have sailed for the towers of the land of Iolcos,
Her heart on fire with passionate love for Jason;
Nor would she have persuaded the daughters of Pelias
To kill their father, and now be living here
In Corinth with her husband and children. She gave
Pleasure to the people of her land of exile,
And she herself helped Jason in every way.
This is indeed the greatest salvation of all,—
For the wife not to stand apart from the husband.
But now there's hatred everywhere. Love is diseased.
For, deserting his own children and my mistress,
Jason has taken a royal wife to his bed,
The daughter of the ruler of this land, Kreon.
And poor Medea is slighted, and cries aloud on the
Vows they made to each other, the right hands clasped
In eternal promise. She calls upon the gods to witness
What sort of return Jason has made to her love.
She lies without food and gives herself up to suffering,
Wasting away every moment of the day in tears.
So it has gone since she knew herself slighted by him.
Not stirring an eye, not moving her face from the ground,
No more than either a rock or surging sea water
She listens when she is given friendly advice.

Except that sometimes she twists back her white neck and
Moans to herself, calling out on her father's name,
And her land, and her home betrayed when she came away with
A man who now is determined to dishonour her.
Poor creature, she has discovered by her sufferings
What it means to one not to have lost one's own country.
She has turned from the children and does not like to see them.
I am afraid she may think of some dreadful thing,
For her heart is violent. She will never put up with
The treatment she is getting. I know and fear her
Lest she may sharpen a sword and thrust to the heart,
Stealing into the palace where the bed is made,
Or even kill the king and the new-wedded groom,
And thus bring a greater misfortune on herself.
She's a strange woman. I know it won't be easy
To make an enemy of her and come off best.
But here the children come. They have finished playing.
They have no thought at all of their mother's trouble.
Indeed it is not usual for the young to grieve.

[*Enter from the right the slave who is the tutor to Medea's two small children. The children follow him.*]

TUTOR

You old retainer of my mistress's household,
Why are you standing here all alone in front of the
Gates and moaning to yourself over your misfortune?
Medea could not wish you to leave her alone.

NURSE

Old man, and guardian of the children of Jason,
If one is a good servant, it's a terrible thing
When one's master's luck is out; it goes to one's heart.
So I myself have got into such a state of grief
That a longing stole over me to come outside here
And tell the earth and air of my mistress's sorrows.

TUTOR

Has the poor lady not yet given up her crying?

**NURSE**

Given up? She's at the start, not half-way through her
tears.

**TUTOR**

Poor fool,—if I may call my mistress such a name,—
How ignorant she is of trouble more to come.

**NURSE**

What do you mean, old man? You needn't fear to speak.

**TUTOR**

Nothing. I take back the words which I used just now.

**NURSE**

Don't, by your beard, hide this from me, your fellow-
servant.
If need be, I'll keep quiet about what you tell me.

**TUTOR**

I heard a person saying, while I myself seemed
Not to be paying attention, when I was at the place
Where the old draught-players sit, by the holy fountain,
That Kreon, ruler of the land, intends to drive
These children and their mother in exile from Corinth.
But whether what he said is really true or not
I do not know. I pray that it may not be true.

**NURSE**

And will Jason put up with it that his children
Should suffer so, though he's no friend to their mother?

**TUTOR**

Old ties give place to new ones. As for Jason, he
No longer has a feeling for this house of ours.

**NURSE**

It's black indeed for us, when we add new to old
Sorrows before even the present sky has cleared.

**TUTOR**

But you be silent, and keep all this to yourself.
It is not the right time to tell our mistress of it.

**NURSE**

Do you hear, children, what a father he is to you?

I wish he were dead,—but no, he is still my master.
Yet certainly he has proved unkind to his dear ones.

TUTOR

What's strange in that? Have you only just discovered
That everyone loves himself more than his neighbour?
Some have good reason, others get something out of it.
So Jason neglects his children for the new bride.

NURSE

Go indoors, children. That will be the best thing.
And you, keep them to themselves as much as possible.
Don't bring them near their mother in her angry mood.
For I've seen her already blazing her eyes at them
As though she meant some mischief and I am sure that
She'll not stop raging until she has struck at someone.
May it be an enemy and not a friend she hurts!

[*Medea is heard inside the house.*]

MEDEA

Ah, wretch! Ah, lost in my sufferings,
I wish, I wish I might die.

NURSE

What did I say, dear children? Your mother
Frets her heart and frets it to anger.
Run away quickly into the house,
And keep well out of her sight.
Don't go anywhere near, but be careful
Of the wildness and bitter nature
Of that proud mind.
Go now! Run quickly indoors.
It is clear that she soon will put lightning
In that cloud of her cries that is rising
With a passion increasing. Oh, what will she do,
Proud-hearted and not to be checked on her course,
A soul bitten into with wrong?

[*The Tutor takes the children into the house.*]

MEDEA

Ah, I have suffered
What should be wept for bitterly. I hate you,
Children of a hateful mother. I curse you

29

And your father. Let the whole house crash.

Ah, I pity you, you poor creature.
How can your children share in their father's
Wickedness? Why do you hate them? Oh children,
How much I fear that something may happen!
Great people's tempers are terrible, always
Having their own way, seldom checked,
Dangerous they shift from mood to mood.
How much better to have been accustomed
To live on equal terms with one's neighbours.
I would like to be safe and grow old in a
Humble way. What is moderate sounds best,
Also in practice *is* best for everyone.
Greatness brings no profit to people.
God indeed, when in anger, brings
Greater ruin to great men's houses.

> [*Enter, on the right, a Chorus of Corinthian
> women. They have come to enquire about Me-
> dea and to attempt to console her.*]

**CHORUS**
I heard the voice, I heard the cry
Of Colchis' wretched daughter.
Tell me, mother, is she not yet
At rest? Within the double gates
Of the court I heard her cry. I am sorry
For the sorrow of this home. O, say, what has happened?

**NURSE**
There is no home. It's over and done with.
Her husband holds fast to his royal wedding,
While she, my mistress, cries out her eyes
There in her room, and takes no warmth from
Any word of any friend.

**MEDEA**
Oh, I wish
That lightning from heaven would split my head open.
Oh, what use have I now for life?
I would find my release in death
And leave hateful existence behind me.

O God and Earth and Heaven!
Did you hear what a cry was that
Which the sad wife sings?
Poor foolish one, why should you long
For that appalling rest?
The final end of death comes fast.
No need to pray for that.
Suppose your man gives honour
To another woman's bed.
It often happens. Don't be hurt.
God will be your friend in this.
You must not waste away
Grieving too much for him who shared your bed.

MEDEA

Great Themis, lady Artemis, behold
The things I suffer, though I made him promise,
My hateful husband. I pray that I may see him,
Him and his bride and all their palace shattered
For the wrong they dare to do me without cause.
Oh, my father! Oh, my country! In what dishonour
I left you, killing my own brother for it.

NURSE

Do you hear what she says, and how she cries
On Themis, the goddess of Promises, and on Zeus,
Whom we believe to be the Keeper of Oaths?
Of this I am sure, that no small thing
Will appease my mistress's anger.

CHORUS

Will she come into our presence?
Will she listen when we are speaking
To the word we say?
I wish she might relax her rage
And temper of her heart.
My willingness to help will never
Be wanting to my friends.
But go inside and bring her
Out of the house to us,
And speak kindly to her: hurry,

31

Before she wrongs her own.
This passion of hers moves to something great.

NURSE

I will, but I doubt if I'll manage
to win my mistress over.
But still I'll attempt it to please you.
Such a look she will flash on her servants
If any comes near with a message,
Like a lioness guarding her cubs.
It is right, I think, to consider
Both stupid and lacking in foresight
Those poets of old who wrote songs
For revels and dinners and banquets,
Pleasant sounds for men living at ease;
But none of them all has discovered
How to put to an end with their singing
Or musical instruments grief,
Bitter grief, from which death and disaster
Cheat the hopes of a house. Yet how good
If music could cure men of this! But why raise
To no purpose the voice at a banquet? For *there is*
Already abundance of pleasure for men
With a joy of its own.

[*The Nurse goes into the house.*]

CHORUS

I heard a shriek that is laden with sorrow.
Shrilling out her hard grief she cries out
Upon him who betrayed both her bed and her marriage.
Wronged, she calls on the gods,
On the justice of Zeus, the oath sworn,
Which brought her away
To the opposite shore of the Greeks
Through the gloomy salt straits to the gateway
Of the salty unlimited sea.

[*Medea, attended by servants, comes out of the house.*]

MEDEA

Women of Corinth, I have come outside to you

32

Lest you should be indignant with me; for I know
That many people are overproud, some when alone,
And others when in company. And those who live
Quietly, as I do, get a bad reputation.
For a just judgement is not evident in the eyes
When a man at first sight hates another, before
Learning his character, being in no way injured;
And a foreigner especially must adapt himself.
I'd not approve of even a fellow-countryman
Who by pride and want of manners offends his neigh-
    bours.
But on me this thing has fallen so unexpectedly,
It has broken my heart. I am finished. I let go
All my life's joy. My friends, I only want to die.
It was everything to me to think well of one man,
And he, my own husband, has turned out wholly vile.
Of all things which are living and can form a judgement
We women are the most unfortunate creatures.
Firstly, with an excess of wealth it is required
For us to buy a husband and take for our bodies
A master; for not to take one is even worse.
And now the question is serious whether we take
A good or bad one; for there is no easy escape
For a woman, nor can she say no to her marriage.
She arrives among new modes of behaviour and manners,
And needs prophetic power, unless she has learnt at
    home,
How best to manage him who shares the bed with her.
And if we work out all this well and carefully,
And the husband lives with us and lightly bears his yoke,
Then life is enviable. If not, I'd rather die.
A man, when he's tired of the company in his home,
Goes out of the house and puts an end to his boredom
And turns to a friend or companion of his own age.
But we are forced to keep our eyes on one alone.
What they say of us is that we have a peaceful time
Living at home, while they do the fighting in war.
How wrong they are! I would very much rather stand
Three times in the front of battle than bear one child.
Yet what applies to me does not apply to you.
You have a country. Your family home is here.

You enjoy life and the company of your friends.
But I am deserted, a refugee, thought nothing of
By my husband,—something he won in a foreign land.
I have no mother or brother, nor any relation
With whom I can take refuge in this sea of woe.
This much then is the service I would beg from you:
If I can find the means or devise any scheme
To pay my husband back for what he has done to me,—
Him and his father-in-law and the girl who married
    him,—
Just to keep silent. For in other ways a woman
Is full of fear, defenceless, dreads the sight of cold
Steel; but, when once she is wronged in the matter of
    love,
No other soul can hold so many thoughts of blood.

CHORUS

This I will promise. You are in the right, Medea,
In paying your husband back. I am not surprised at you
For being sad.
             But look! I see our king Kreon
Approaching. He will tell us of some new plan.

   [*Enter, from the right, Kreon, with attendants.*]

KREON

You, with that angry look, so set against your husband,
Medea, I order you to leave my territories
An exile, and take along with you your two children,
And not to waste time doing it. It is my decree,
And I will see it done. I will not return home
Until you are cast from the boundaries of my land.

MEDEA

Oh, this is the end for me. I am utterly lost.
Now I am in the full force of the storm of hate
And have no harbour from ruin to reach easily.
Yet still, in spite of it all, I'll ask the question:
What is your reason, Kreon, for banishing me?

KREON

I am afraid of you,—why should I dissemble it?—
Afraid that you may injure my daughter mortally.
Many things accumulate to support my feeling.

34

You are a clever woman, versed in evil arts,
And are angry at having lost your husband's love.
I hear that you are threatening, so they tell me,
To do something against my daughter and Jason
And me, too. I shall take my precautions first.
I tell you, I prefer to earn your hatred now
Than to be soft-hearted and afterwards regret it.

MEDEA

This is not the first time, Kreon. Often previously
Through being considered clever I have suffered much.
A person of sense ought never to have his children
Brought up to be more clever than the average.
For, apart from cleverness bringing them no profit,
It will make them objects of envy and ill-will.
If you put new ideas before the eyes of fools
They'll think you foolish and worthless into the bargain;
And if you are thought superior to those who have
Some reputation for learning, you will become hated.
I have some knowledge myself of how this happens;
For being clever, I find that some will envy me,
Others object to me. Yet all my cleverness
Is not so much.
                    Well, then, are you frightened, Kreon,
That I should harm you? There is no need. It is not
My way to transgress the authority of a king.
How have you injured me? You gave your daughter
     away
To the man you wanted. O, certainly I hate
My husband, but you, I think, have acted wisely;
Nor do I grudge it you that your affairs go well.
May the marriage be a lucky one! Only let me
Live in this land. For even though I have been wronged,
I will not raise my voice, but submit to my betters.

KREON

What you say sounds gentle enough. Still in my heart
I greatly dread that you are plotting some evil,
And therefore I trust you even less than before.
A sharp-tempered woman, or for that matter a man,
Is easier to deal with than the clever type

35

Who holds her tongue. No. You must go. No need for
  more
Speeches. The thing is fixed. By no manner of means
Shall you, an enemy of mine, stay in my country.

MEDEA

I beg you. By your knees, by your new-wedded girl.

KREON

Your words are wasted. You will never persuade me.

MEDEA

Will you drive me out, and give no heed to my prayers?

KREON

I will, for I love my family more than you.

MEDEA

O my country! How bitterly now I remember you!

KREON

I love my country too,—next after my children.

MEDEA

O what an evil to men is passionate love!

KREON

That would depend on the luck that goes along with it.

MEDEA

O God, do not forget who is the cause of this!

KREON

Go. It is no use. Spare me the pain of forcing you.

MEDEA

I'm spared no pain. I lack no pain to be spared me.

KREON

Then you'll be removed by force by one of my men.

MEDEA

No, Kreon, not that! But do listen, I beg you.

KREON

Woman, you seem to want to create a disturbance.

MEDEA

I *will* go into exile. *This* is not what I beg for.

Why then this violence and clinging to my hand?

MEDEA

Allow me to remain here just for this one day,
So I may consider where to live in my exile,
And look for support for my children, since their father
Chooses to make no kind of provision for them.
Have pity on them! You have children of your own.
It is natural for you to look kindly on them.
For myself I do not mind if I go into exile.
It is the children being in trouble that I mind.

KREON

There is nothing tyrannical about my nature,
And by showing mercy I have often been the loser.
Even now I know that I am making a mistake.
All the same you shall have your will. But this I tell you,
That if the light of heaven tomorrow shall see you,
You and your children in the confines of my land,
You die. This word I have spoken is firmly fixed.
But now, if you must stay, stay for this day alone.
For in it you can do none of the things I fear.

[*Exit Kreon with his attendants.*]

CHORUS

Oh, unfortunate one! Oh, cruel!
Where will you turn? Who will help you?
What house or what land to preserve you
From ill can you find?
Medea, a god has thrown suffering
Upon you in waves of despair.

MEDEA

Things have gone badly every way. No doubt of that.
But not these things this far, and don't imagine so.
There are still trials to come for the new-wedded pair,
And for their relations pain that will mean something.
Do you think that I would ever have fawned on that man
Unless I had some end to gain or profit in it?
I would not even have spoken or touched him with my
    hands.
But he has got to such a pitch of foolishness

37

That, though he could have made nothing of all my plans
By exiling me, he has given me this one day
To stay here, and in this I will make dead bodies
Of three of my enemies,—father, the girl and my hus-
    band.
I have many ways of death which I might suit to them,
And do not know, friends, which one to take in hand;
Whether to set fire underneath their bridal mansion,
Or sharpen a sword and thrust it to the heart,
Stealing into the palace where the bed is made.
There is just one obstacle to this. If I am caught
Breaking into the house and scheming against it,
I shall die, and give my enemies cause for laughter.
It is best to go by the straight road, the one in which
I am most skilled, and make away with them by poison.
So be it then.
And now suppose them dead. What town will receive
    me?
What friend will offer me a refuge in his land,
Or the guarantee of his house and save my own life?
There is none. So I must wait a little time yet,
And if some sure defence should then appear for me,
In craft and silence I will set about this murder.
But if my fate should drive me on without help,
Even though death is certain, I will take the sword
Myself and kill, and steadfastly advance to crime.
It shall not be,—I swear it by her, my mistress,
Whom most I honour and have chosen as partner,
Hecate, who dwells in the recesses of my hearth,—
That any man shall be glad to have injured me.
Bitter I will make their marriage for them and mournful,
Bitter the alliance and the driving me out of the land.
Ah, come, Medea, in your plotting and scheming
Leave nothing untried of all those things which you
    know.
Go forward to the dreadful act. The test has come
For resolution. You see how you are treated. Never
Shall you be mocked by Jason's Corinthian wedding,
Whose father was noble, whose grandfather Helios.
You have the skill. What is more, you were born a
    woman,

And women, though most helpless in doing good deeds,
Are of every evil the cleverest of contrivers.

CHORUS
Flow backward to your sources, sacred rivers,
And let the world's great order be reversed.
It is the thoughts of *men* that are deceitful,
*Their* pledges that are loose.
Story shall now turn my condition to a fair one,
Women are paid their due.
No more shall evil-sounding fame be theirs.

Cease now, you muses of the ancient singers,
To tell the tale of my unfaithfulness;
For not on us did Phoebus, lord of music,
Bestow the lyre's divine
Power, for otherwise I should have sung an answer
To the other sex. Long time
Has much to tell of us, and much of them.

You sailed away from your father's home,
With a heart on fire you passed
The double rocks of the sea.
And now in a foreign country
You have lost your rest in a widowed bed,
And are driven forth, a refugee
In dishonour from the land.

Good faith has gone, and no more remains
In great Greece a sense of shame.
It has flown away to the sky.
No father's house for a haven
Is at hand for you now, and another queen
Of your bed has dispossessed you and
Is mistress of your home.

[*Enter Jason, with attendants.*]

JASON
This is not the first occasion that I have noticed
How hopeless it is to deal with a stubborn temper.
For, with reasonable submission to our ruler's will,

You might have lived in this land and kept your home.
As it is you are going to be exiled for your loose speak-
    ing.
Not that I mind myself. You are free to continue
Telling everyone that Jason is a worthless man.
But as to your talk about the king, consider
Yourself most lucky that exile is your punishment.
I, for my part, have always tried to calm down
The anger of the king, and wished you to remain.
But you will not give up your folly, continually
Speaking ill of him, and so you are going to be banished.
All the same, and in spite of your conduct, I'll not desert
My friends, but have come to make some provision for
    you,
So that you and the children may not be penniless
Or in need of anything in exile. Certainly
Exile brings many troubles with it. And even
If you hate me, I cannot think badly of you.

MEDEA

O coward in every way,—that is what I call you,
With bitterest reproach for your lack of manliness,
You have come, you, my worst enemy, have come to me!
It is not an example of over-confidence
Or of boldness thus to look your friends in the face,
Friends you have injured,—no, it is the worst of all
Human diseases, shamelessness. But you did well
To come, for I can speak ill of you and lighten
My heart, and you will suffer while you are listening.
And first I will begin from what happened first.
I saved your life, and every Greek knows I saved it,
Who was a ship-mate of yours aboard the Argo,
When you were sent to control the bulls that breathed
    fire
And yoke them, and when you would sow that deadly
    field.
Also that snake, who encircled with his many folds
The Golden Fleece and guarded it and never slept,
I killed, and so gave you the safety of the light.
And I myself betrayed my father and my home,
And came with you to Pelias' land of Iolcos.

40

And then, showing more willingness to help than wisdom,
I killed him, Pelias, with a most dreadful death
At his own daughters' hands, and took away your fear.
This is how I behaved to you, you wretched man,
And you forsook me, took another bride to bed
Though you had children; for, if that had not been,
You would have had an excuse for another wedding.
Faith in your word has gone. Indeed I cannot tell
Whether you think the gods whose names you swore by
    then
Have ceased to rule and that new standards are set up,
Since you must know you have broken your word to me.
O my right hand, and the knees which you often clasped
In supplication, how senselessly I am treated
By this bad man, and how my hopes have missed their
    mark!
Come, I will share my thoughts as though you were a
    friend,—
You! Can I think that you would ever treat me well?
But I will do it, and these questions will make you
Appear the baser. Where am I to go? To my father's?
Him I betrayed and his land when I came with you.
To Pelias' wretched daughters? What a fine welcome
They would prepare for me who murdered their father!
For this is my position,—hated by my friends
At home, I have, in kindness to you, made enemies
Of others whom there was no need to have injured.
And how happy among Greek women you have made me
On your side for all this! A distinguished husband
I have,—for breaking promises. When in misery
I am cast out of the land and go into exile,
Quite without friends and all alone with my children,
That will be a fine shame for the new-wedded groom,
For his children to wander as beggars and she who saved
    him.
O God, you have given to mortals a sure method
Of telling the gold that is pure from the counterfeit;
Why is there no mark engraved upon men's bodies,
By which we could know the true ones from the false
    ones?

It is a strange form of anger, difficult to cure
When two friends turn upon each other in hatred.

JASON

As for me, it seems I must be no bad speaker.
But, like a man who has a good grip of the tiller,
Reef up his sail, and so run away from under
This mouthing tempest, woman, of your bitter tongue.
Since you insist on building up your kindness to me,
My view is that Cypris was alone responsible
Of men and gods for the preserving of my life.
You are clever enough,—but really I need not enter
Into the story of how it was love's inescapable
Power that compelled you to keep my person safe.
On this I will not go into too much detail.
In so far as you helped me, you did well enough.
But on this question of saving me, I can prove
You have certainly got from me more than you gave.
Firstly, instead of living among barbarians,
You inhabit a Greek land and understand our ways,
How to live by law instead of the sweet will of force.
And all the Greeks considered you a clever woman.
You were honoured for it; while, if you were living at
The ends of the earth, nobody would have heard of you.
For my part, rather than stores of gold in my house
Or power to sing even sweeter songs than Orpheus,
I'd choose the fate that made me a distinguished man.
There is my reply to your story of my labours.
Remember it was you who started the argument.
Next for your attack on my wedding with the princess:
Here I will prove that, first, it was a clever move,
Secondly, a wise one, and, finally, that I made it
In your best interests and the children's. Please keep
  calm.
When I arrived here from the land of Iolcos,
Involved, as I was, in every kind of difficulty,
What luckier chance could I have come across than this,
An exile to marry the daughter of the king?
It was not,—the point that seems to upset you—that I
Grew tired of your bed and felt the need of a new bride;

42

Nor with any wish to outdo your number of children.
We have enough already. I am quite content.
But,—this was the main reason—that we might live well,
And not be short of anything. I know that all
A man's friends leave him stone-cold if he becomes poor.
Also that I might bring my children up worthily
Of my position, and, by producing more of them
To be brothers of yours, we would draw the families
Together and all be happy. You need no children.
And it pays me to do good to those I have now
By having others. Do you think this a bad plan?
You wouldn't if the love question hadn't upset you.
But you women have got into such a state of mind
That, if your life at night is good, you think you have
Everything; but, if in that quarter things go wrong,
You will consider your best and truest interests
Most hateful. It would have been better far for men
To have got their children in some other way, and
    women
Not to have existed. Then life would have been good.

### CHORUS

Jason, though you have made this speech of yours look
    well,
Still I think, even though others do not agree,
You have betrayed your wife and are acting badly.

### MEDEA

Surely in many ways I hold different views
From others, for I think that the plausible speaker
Who is a villain deserves the greatest punishment.
Confident in his tongue's power to adorn evil,
He stops at nothing. Yet he is not really wise.
As in your case. There is no need to put on the airs
Of a clever speaker, for one word will lay you flat.
If you were not a coward, you would not have married
Behind my back, but discussed it with me first.

### JASON

And you, no doubt, would have furthered the proposal,
If I had told you of it, you who even now
Are incapable of controlling your bitter temper.

#### MEDEA

It was not that. No, you thought it was not respectable
As you got on in years to have a foreign wife.

#### JASON

Make sure of this: it was not because of a woman
I made the royal alliance in which I now live,
But, as I said before, I wished to preserve you
And breed a royal progeny to be brothers
To the children I have now, a sure defence to us.

#### MEDEA

Let me have no happy fortune that brings pain with it,
Or prosperity which is upsetting to the mind!

#### JASON

Change your ideas of what you want, and show more
   sense.
Do not consider painful what is good for you,
Nor, when you are lucky, think yourself unfortunate.

#### MEDEA

You can insult me. You have somewhere to turn to.
But I shall go from this land into exile, friendless.

#### JASON

It was what you chose yourself. Don't blame others for it.

#### MEDEA

And how did I choose it? Did I betray my husband?

#### JASON

You called down wicked curses on the king's family.

#### MEDEA

A curse, that is what I am become to your house too.

#### JASON

I do not propose to go into all the rest of it;
But, if you wish for the children or for yourself
In exile to have some of my money to help you,
Say so, for I am prepared to give with open hand,
Or to provide you with introductions to my friends
Who will treat you well. You are a fool if you do not
Accept this. Cease your anger and you will profit.

## MEDEA

I shall never accept the favours of friends of yours,
Nor take a thing from you, so you need not offer it.
There is no benefit in the gifts of a bad man.

## JASON

Then, in any case, I call the gods to witness that
I wish to help you and the children in every way,
But you refuse what is good for you. Obstinately
You push away your friends. You are sure to suffer for it.

## MEDEA

Go! No doubt you hanker for your virginal bride,
And are guilty of lingering too long out of her house.
Enjoy your wedding. But perhaps,—with the help of
       God—
You will make the kind of marriage that you will regret.
                    [*Jason goes out with his attendants.*]

## CHORUS

When love is in excess
It brings a man no honour
Nor any worthiness.
But if in moderation Cypris comes,
There is no other power at all so gracious.
O goddess, never on me let loose the unerring
Shaft of your bow in the poison of desire.

Let my heart be wise.
It is the gods' best gift.
On me let mighty Cypris
Inflict no wordy wars or restless anger
To urge my passion to a different love.
But with discernment may she guide women's weddings,
Honouring most what is peaceful in the bed.

O country and home,
Never, never may I be without you,
Living the hopeless life,
Hard to pass through and painful,
Most pitiable of all.
Let death first lay me low and death

45

Free me from this daylight.
There is no sorrow above
The loss of a native land.

I have seen it myself,
Do not tell of a secondhand story.
Neither city nor friend
Pitied you when you suffered
The worst of sufferings.
O let him die ungraced whose heart
Will not reward his friends,
Who cannot open an honest mind
No friend will he be of mine.

> [Enter Aigeus, king of Athens, and old friend
> of Medea.]

AIGEUS

Medea, greeting! This is the best introduction
Of which men know for conversation between friends.

MEDEA

Greeting to you too, Aigeus, son of King Pandion,
Where have you come from to visit this country's soil?

AIGEUS

I have just left the ancient oracle of Phoebus.

MEDEA

And why did you go to earth's prophetic centre?

AIGEUS

I went to inquire how children might be born to me.

MEDEA

Is it so? Your life still up to this point childless?

AIGEUS

Yes. By the fate of some power we have no children.

MEDEA

Have you a wife, or is there none to share your bed?

AIGEUS

There is. Yes, I am joined to my wife in marriage.

MEDEA

And what did Phoebus say to you about children?

46

AIGEUS

Words too wise for a mere man to guess their meaning.

MEDEA

Is it proper for me to be told the god's reply?

AIGEUS

It is. For sure what is needed is cleverness.

MEDEA

Then what was his message? Tell me, if I may hear.

AIGEUS

I am not to loosen the hanging foot of the wine-skin . . .

MEDEA

Until you have done something, or reached some country?

AIGEUS

Until I return again to my hearth and house.

MEDEA

And for what purpose have you journeyed to this land?

AIGEUS

There is a man called Pittheus, king of Troezen.

MEDEA

A son of Pelops, they say, a most righteous man.

AIGEUS

With him I wish to discuss the reply of the god.

MEDEA

Yes. He is wise and experienced in such matters.

AIGEUS

And to me also the dearest of all my spear-friends.

MEDEA

Well, I hope you have good luck, and achieve your will.

AIGEUS

But why this downcast eye of yours, and this pale cheek?

MEDEA

O Aigeus, my husband has been the worst of all to me.

AIGEUS

What do you mean? Say clearly what has caused this
grief.

**MEDEA**

Jason wrongs me, though I have never injured him.

**AIGEUS**

What has he done? Tell me about it in clearer words.

**MEDEA**

He has taken a wife to his house, supplanting me.

**AIGEUS**

Surely he would not dare to do a thing like that.

**MEDEA**

Be sure he has. Once dear, I now am slighted by him.

**AIGEUS**

Did he fall in love? Or is he tired of your love?

**MEDEA**

He was greatly in love, this traitor to his friends.

**AIGEUS**

Then let him go, if, as you say, he's so bad.

**MEDEA**

A passionate love,—for an alliance with the king.

**AIGEUS**

And who gave him his wife? Tell me the rest of it.

**MEDEA**

It was Kreon, he who rules this land of Corinth.

**AIGEUS**

Indeed, Medea, your grief was understandable.

**MEDEA**

I am ruined. And there is more to come: I am banished.

**AIGEUS**

Banished? By whom? Here you tell me of a new wrong.

**MEDEA**

Kreon drives me an exile from the land of Corinth.

**AIGEUS**

Does Jason consent? I cannot approve of this.

**MEDEA**

He pretends not to, but he will put up with it.
Ah, Aigeus, I beg and beseech you, by your beard

And by your knees I am making myself your suppliant,
Have pity on me, have pity on your poor friend,
And do not let me go into exile desolate,
But receive me in your land and at your very hearth.
So may your love, with God's help, lead to the bearing
Of children, and so may you yourself die happy.
You do not know what a chance you have come on here.
I will end your childlessness, and I will make you able
To beget children. The drugs I know can do this.

AIGEUS

For many reasons, woman, I am anxious to do
This favour for you. First, for the sake of the gods,
And then for the birth of children which you promise,
For in that respect I am entirely at my wits' end.
But this is my position: if you reach my land,
I, being in my rights, will try to befriend you.
But this much I must warn you of beforehand:
I shall not agree to take you out of this country;
But if you by yourself can reach my house, then you
Shall stay there safely. To none will I give you up.
But from this land you must make your escape yourself,
For I do not wish to incur blame from my friends.

MEDEA

It shall be so. But, if I might have a pledge from you
For this, then I would have from you all I desire.

AIGEUS

Do you not trust me? What is it rankles with you?

MEDEA

I trust you, yes. But the house of Pelias hates me,
And so does Kreon. If you are bound by this oath,
When they try to drag me from your land, you will not
Abandon me; but if our pact is only words,
With no oath to the gods, you will be lightly armed,
Unable to resist their summons. I am weak,
While they have wealth to help them and a royal house.

AIGEUS

You show much foresight for such negotiations.
Well, if you will have it so, I will not refuse.
For, both on my side this will be the safest way

49

To have some excuse to put forward to your enemies,
And for you it is more certain. You may name the gods.

MEDEA

Swear by the plain of Earth, and Helios, father
Of my father, and name together all the gods. . . .

AIGEUS

That I will act or not act in what way? Speak.

MEDEA

That you yourself will never cast me from your land,
Nor, if any of my enemies should demand me,
Will you, in your life, willingly hand me over.

AIGEUS

I swear by the Earth, by the holy light of Helios,
By all the gods, I will abide by this you say.

MEDEA

Enough. And, if you fail, what shall happen to you?

AIGEUS

What comes to those who have no regard for heaven.

MEDEA

Go on your way. Farewell. For I am satisfied,
And I will reach your city as soon as I can,
Having done the deed I have to do and gained my end.

[*Aigeus goes out.*]

CHORUS

May Hermes, god of travellers,
Escort you, Aigeus, to your home!
And may you have the things you wish
So eagerly; for you
Appear to me to be a generous man.

MEDEA

God, and God's daughter, justice, and light of Helios!
Now, friends, has come the time of my triumph over
My enemies, and now my foot is on the road.
Now I am confident they will pay the penalty.
For this man, Aigeus, has been like a harbour to me
In all my plans just where I was most distressed.
To him I can fasten the cable of my safety

50

When I have reached the town and fortress of Pallas.
And now I shall tell to you the whole of my plan.
Listen to these words that are not spoken idly.
I shall send one of my servants to find Jason
And request him to come once more into my sight.
And when he comes, the words I'll say will be soft ones.
I'll say that I agree with him, that I approve
The royal wedding he has made, betraying me.
I'll say it was profitable, an excellent idea.
But I shall beg that my children may remain here:
Not that I would leave in a country that hates me
Children of mine to feel their enemies' insults,
But that by a trick I may kill the king's daughter.
For I will send the children with gifts in their hands
To carry to the bride, so as not to be banished,—
A finely woven dress and a golden diadem.
And if she takes them and wears them upon her skin
She and all who touch the girl will die in agony;
Such poison will I lay upon the gifts I send.
But there, however, I must leave that account paid.
I weep to think of what a deed I have to do
Next after that; for I shall kill my own children.
My children, there is none who can give them safety.
And when I have ruined the whole of Jason's house,
I shall leave the land and flee from the murder of my
Dear children, and I shall have done a dreadful deed.
For it is not bearable to be mocked by enemies.
So it must happen. What profit have I in life?
I have no land, no home, no refuge from my pain.
My mistake was made the time I left behind me
My father's house, and trusted the words of a Greek,
Who, with heaven's help, will pay me the price for that.
For those children he had from me he will never
See alive again, nor will he on his new bride
Beget another child, for she is to be forced
To die a most terrible death by these my poisons.
Let no one think me a weak one, feeble-spirited,
A stay-at-home, but rather just the opposite,
One who can hurt my enemies and help my friends;
For the lives of such persons are most remembered.

**CHORUS**

Since you have shared the knowledge of your plans with
   us,
I both wish to help you and support the normal
Ways of mankind, and tell you not to do this thing.

**MEDEA**

I can do no other thing. It is understandable
For you to speak thus. You have not suffered as I have.

**CHORUS**

But can you have the heart to kill your flesh and blood?

**MEDEA**

Yes, for this is the best way to wound my husband.

**CHORUS**

And you too. Of women you will be most unhappy.

**MEDEA**

So it must be. No compromise is possible.

[*She turns to the Nurse.*]

Go, you, at once, and tell Jason to come to me.
You I employ on all affairs of greatest trust.
Say nothing of these decisions which I have made,
If you love your mistress, if you were born a woman.

**CHORUS**

From of old the children of Erechtheus are
Splendid, the sons of blessed gods. They dwell
In Athens' holy and unconquered land,
Where famous Wisdom feeds them and they pass gaily
Always through that most brilliant air where once, they
   say,
That golden Harmony gave birth to the nine
Pure Muses of Pieria.

And beside the sweet flow of Cephisos' stream,
Where Cypris sailed, they say, to draw the water,
And mild soft breezes breathed along her path,
And on her hair were flung the sweet-smelling garlands
Of flowers of roses by the Lovers, the companions

Of Wisdom, her escort, the helpers of men
In every kind of excellence.

How then can these holy rivers
Or this holy land love you,
Or the city find you a home,
You, who will kill your children,
You, not pure with the rest?
O think of the blow at your children
And think of the blood that you shed.
O, over and over I beg you,
By your knees I beg you do not
Be the murderess of your babes!

O where will you find the courage
Or the skill of hand and heart,
When you set yourself to attempt
A deed so dreadful to do?
How, when you look upon them,
Can you tearlessly hold the decision
For murder? You will not be able,
When your children fall down and implore you,
You will not be able to dip
Steadfast your hand in their blood.

[*Enter Jason with attendants.*]

JASON

I have come at your request. Indeed, although you are
Bitter against me, this you shall have: I will listen
To what new thing you want, woman, to get from me.

MEDEA

Jason, I beg you to be forgiving towards me
For what I said. It is natural for you to bear with
My temper, since we have had much love together.
I have talked with myself about this and I have
Reproached myself. 'Fool,' I said, 'why am I so mad?
Why am I set against those who have planned wisely?
Why make myself an enemy of the authorities
And of my husband, who does the best thing for me
By marrying royalty and having children who
Will be as brothers to my own? What is wrong with me?

53

Let me give up anger, for the gods are kind to me.
Have I not children, and do I not know that we
In exile from our country must be short of friends?'
When I considered this I saw that I had shown
Great lack of sense, and that my anger was foolish. Now
I agree with you. I think that you are wise
In having this other wife as well as me, and I
Was mad. I should have helped you in these plans of
    yours,
Have joined in the wedding, stood by the marriage bed,
Have taken pleasure in attendance on your bride.
But we women are what we are,—perhaps a little
Worthless; and you men must not be like us in this,
Nor be foolish in return when we are foolish.
Now I give in, and admit that then I was wrong.
I have come to a better understanding now.

[She turns towards the house.]

Children, come here, my children, come outdoors to us!
Welcome your father with me, and say goodbye to him,
And with your mother, who just now was his enemy,
Join again in making friends with him who loves us.

[Enter the children, attended by the Tutor.]

We have made peace, and all our anger is over.
Take hold of his right hand,—O God, I am thinking
Of something which may happen in a secret future.
O children, will you just so, after a long life,
Hold out your loving arms at the grave? O children,
How ready to cry I am, how full of foreboding!
I am ending at last this quarrel with your father,
And, look, my soft eyes have suddenly filled with tears.

CHORUS

And the pale tears have started also in my eyes.
O may the trouble not grow worse than now it is!

JASON

I approve of what you say. And I cannot blame you
Even for what you said before. It is natural
For a woman to be wild with her husband when he
Goes in for secret love. But now your mind has turned
To better reasoning. In the end you have come to

54

The right decision, like the clever woman you are.
And of you, children, your father is taking care.
He has made, with God's help, ample provision for you.
For I think that a time will come when you will be
The leading people in Corinth with your brothers.
You must grow up. As to the future, your father
And those of the gods who love him will deal with that.
I want to see you, when you have become young men,
Healthy and strong, better men than my enemies.
Medea, why are your eyes all wet with pale tears?
Why is your cheek so white and turned away from me?
Are not these words of mine pleasing for you to hear?

MEDEA

It is nothing. I was thinking about these children.

JASON

You must be cheerful. I shall look after them well.

MEDEA

I will be. It is not that I distrust your words,
But a woman is a frail thing, prone to crying.

JASON

But why then should you grieve so much for these
    children?

MEDEA

I am their mother. When you prayed that they might live,
I felt unhappy to think that these things will be.
But come, I have said something of the things I meant
To say to you, and now I will tell you the rest.
Since it is the king's will to banish me from here,—
And for me too I know that this is the best thing,
Not to be in your way by living here or in
The king's way, since they think me ill-disposed to them,—
I then am going into exile from this land;
But do you, so that you may have the care of them,
Beg Kreon that the children may not be banished.

JASON

I doubt if I'll succeed, but I'll attempt it.

MEDEA

Then you must tell your wife to beg from her father

That the children may be reprieved from banishment.

JASON

I will, and with her I shall certainly succeed.

MEDEA

If she is like the rest of us women, you will.
And I too will take a hand with you in this business,
For I will send her some gifts which are far fairer,
I am sure of it, than those which now are in fashion,
A finely-woven dress and a golden diadem,
And the children shall present them. Quick, let one of you
Servants bring here to me that beautiful dress.

[*One of her attendants goes into the house.*]

She will be happy not in one way, but in a hundred,
Having so fine a man as you to share her bed,
And with this beautiful dress which Helios of old,
My father's father, bestowed on his descendants.

[*Enter attendant carrying the poisoned dress and diadem.*]

There, children, take these wedding presents in your hands.
Take them to the royal princess, the happy bride,
And give them to her. She will not think little of them.

JASON

No, don't be foolish, and empty your hands of these.
Do you think the palace is short of dresses to wear?
Do you think there is no gold there? Keep them, don't
give them
Away. If my wife considers me of any value,
She will think more of me than money, I am sure of it.

MEDEA

No, let me have my way. They say the gods themselves
Are moved by gifts, and gold does more with men than
words.
Hers is the luck, her fortune that which god blesses;
She is young and a princess; but for my children's reprieve
I would give my very life, and not gold only.
Go children, go together to that rich palace,
Be suppliants to the new wife of your father,
My lady, beg her not to let you be banished.

And give her the dress,—for this is of great importance,
That she should take the gift into her hand from yours.
Go, quick as you can. And bring your mother good news
By your success of those things which she longs to gain.

*[Jason goes out with his attendants, followed by
the Tutor and the children carrying the poisoned
gifts.]*

### CHORUS

Now there is no hope left for the children's lives.
Now there is none. They are walking already to murder.
The bride, poor bride, will accept the curse of the gold,
Will accept the bright diadem.
Around her yellow hair she will set that dress
Of death with her own hands.
The grace and the perfume and glow of the golden robe
Will charm her to put them upon her and wear the wreath,
And now her wedding will be with the dead below,
Into such a trap she will fall,
Poor thing, into such a fate of death and never
Escape from under that curse.

You too, O wretched bridegroom, making your match
    with kings,
You do not see that you bring
Destruction on your children and on her,
Your wife, a fearful death.
Poor soul, what a fall is yours!

In your grief too I weep, mother of little children,
You who will murder your own,
In vengeance for the loss of married love
Which Jason has betrayed
As he lives with another wife.

*[Enter the Tutor with the children.]*

### TUTOR

Mistress, I tell you that these children are reprieved,
And the royal bride has been pleased to take in her hands
Your gifts. In that quarter the children are secure.
But come,

57

Why do you stand confused when you are fortunate?
Why have you turned round with your cheek away from
　　me?
Are not these words of mine pleasing for you to hear?

MEDEA

Oh! I am lost!

TUTOR

That word is not in harmony with my tidings.

MEDEA

I am lost, I am lost!

TUTOR

　　　　　　　Am I in ignorance telling you
Of some disaster, and not the good news I thought?

MEDEA

You have told what you have told. I do not blame you.

TUTOR

Why then this downcast eye, and this weeping of tears?

MEDEA

Oh, I am forced to weep, old man. The gods and I,
I in a kind of madness have contrived all this.

TUTOR

Courage! You too will be brought home by your children.

MEDEA

Ah, before that happens I shall bring others home.

TUTOR

Others before you have been parted from their children
Mortals must bear in resignation their ill luck.

MEDEA

That is what I shall do. But go inside the house,
And do for the children your usual daily work.

　　[*The Tutor goes into the house. Medea turns
　　to her children.*]

O children, O my children, you have a city,
You have a home, and you can leave me behind you,
And without your mother you may live there for ever.
But I am going in exile to another land

58

Before I have seen you happy and taken pleasure in you,
Before I have dressed your brides and made your mar-
    riage beds,
And held up the torch at the ceremony of wedding.
Oh, what a wretch I am in this my self-willed thought!
What was the purpose, children, for which I reared you?
For all my travail and wearing myself away?
They were sterile, those pains I had in the bearing of you.
O surely once the hopes in you I had, poor me,
Were high ones: you would look after me in old age,
And when I died would deck me well with your own
    hands;
A thing which all would have done. O but now it is gone,
That lovely thought. For, once I am left without you,
Sad will be the life I'll lead and sorrowful for me.
And you will never see your mother again with
Your dear eyes, gone to another mode of living.
Why, children, do you look upon me with your eyes?
Why do you smile so sweetly that last smile of all?
Oh, Oh, what can I do? My spirit has gone from me,
Friends, when I saw that bright look in the children's eyes.
I cannot bear to do it. I renounce my plans
I had before. I'll take my children away from
This land. Why should I hurt their father with the pain
They feel, and suffer twice as much of pain myself?
No, no, I will not do it. I renounce my plans.
Ah, what is wrong with me? Do I want to let go
My enemies unhurt and be laughed at for it?
I must face this thing. Oh, but what a weak woman
Even to admit to my mind these soft arguments.
Children, go into the house. And he whom law forbids
To stand in attendance at my sacrifices,
Let him see to it. I shall not mar my handiwork.
Oh! Oh!
Do not, O my heart, you must not do these things!
Poor heart, let them go, have pity upon the children.
If they live with you in Athens they will cheer you.
No! By Hell's avenging furies it shall not be,—
This shall never be, that I should suffer my children
To be the prey of my enemies' insolence.
Every way is it fixed. The bride will not escape.

No, the diadem is now upon her head, and she,
The royal princess, is dying in the dress, I know it.
But,—for it is the most dreadful of roads for me
To tread, and them I shall send on a more dreadful still—
I wish to speak to the children.

[*She calls the children to her.*]

Come, children, give
Me your hands, give your mother your hands to kiss them.
O the dear hands, and O how dear are these lips to me,
And the generous eyes and the bearing of my children!
I wish you happiness, but not here in this world.
What is here your father took. O how good to hold you!
How delicate the skin, how sweet the breath of children!
Go, go! I am no longer able, no longer
To look upon you. I am overcome by sorrow.

[*The children go into the house.*]

I know indeed what evil I intend to do,
But stronger than all my afterthoughts is my fury,
Fury that brings upon mortals the greatest evils.

[*She goes out to the right, towards the royal palace.*]

**CHORUS**

Often before
I have gone through more subtle reasons,
And have come upon questionings greater
Than a woman should strive to search out.
But we too have a goddess to help us
And accompany us into wisdom.
Not all of us. Still you will find
Among many women a few,
And our sex is not without learning.
This I say, that those who have never
Had children, who know nothing of it,
In happiness have the advantage
Over those who are parents.
The childless, who never discover
Whether children turn out as a good thing
Or as something to cause pain, are spared
Many troubles in lacking this knowledge.

And those who have in their homes
The sweet presence of children, I see that their lives
Are all wasted away by their worries.
First they must think how to bring them up well and
How to leave them something to live on.
And then after this whether all their toil
Is for those who will turn out good or bad,
Is still an unanswered question.
And of one more trouble, the last of all,
That is common to mortals I tell.
For suppose you have found them enough for their living,
Suppose that the children have grown into youth
And have turned out good, still, if God so wills it,
Death will away with your children's bodies,
And carry them off into Hades.
What is our profit, then, that for the sake of
Children the gods should pile upon mortals
After all else
This most terrible grief of all?

[*Enter Medea, from the spectators' right.*]

MEDEA

Friends, I can tell you that for long I have waited
For the event. I stare towards the place from where
The news will come. And now, see one of Jason's servants
Is on his way here, and that laboured breath of his
Shows he has tidings for us, and evil tidings.

[*Enter, also from the right, the Messenger.*]

MESSENGER

Medea, you who have done such a dreadful thing,
So outrageous, run for your life, take what you can,
A ship to bear you hence or chariot on land.

MEDEA

And what is the reason deserves such flight as this?

MESSENGER

She is dead, only just now, the royal princess,
And Kreon dead too, her father, by your poisons.

MEDEA

The finest words you have spoken. Now and hereafter
I shall count you among my benefactors and friends.

61

What! Are you right in the mind? Are you not mad,
Woman? The house of the king is outraged by you.
Do you enjoy it? Not afraid of such doings?

MEDEA

To what you say I on my side have something too
To say in answer. Do not be in a hurry, friend,
But speak. How did they die? You will delight me twice
As much again if you say they died in agony.

MESSENGER

When those two children, born of you, had entered in,
Their father with them, and passed into the bride's house,
We were pleased, we slaves who were distressed by your
      wrongs.
All through the house we were talking of but one thing,
How you and your husband had made up your quarrel.
Some kissed the children's hands and some their yellow
      hair,
And I myself was so full of my joy that I
Followed the children into the women's quarters.
Our mistress, whom we honour now instead of you,
Before she noticed that your two children were there,
Was keeping her eye fixed eagerly on Jason.
Afterwards however she covered up her eyes,
Her cheek paled and she turned herself away from him,
So disgusted was she at the children's coming there.
But your husband tried to end the girl's bad temper,
And said 'You must not look unkindly on your friends.
Cease to be angry. Turn your head to me again.
Have as your friends the same ones as your husband has.
And take these gifts, and beg your father to reprieve
These children from their exile. Do it for my sake.'
She, when she saw the dress, could not restrain herself.
She agreed with all her husband said, and before
He and the children had gone far from the palace,
She took the gorgeous robe and dressed herself in it,
And put the golden crown around her curly locks,
And arranged the set of the hair in a shining mirror,
And smiled at the lifeless image of herself in it.
Then she rose from her chair and walked about the room,

With her gleaming feet stepping most soft and delicate,
All overjoyed with the present. Often and often
She would stretch her foot out straight and look along it.
But after that it was a fearful thing to see.
The colour of her face changed, and she staggered back,
She ran, and her legs trembled, and she only just
Managed to reach a chair without falling flat down.
An aged woman servant who, I take it, thought
This was some seizure of Pan or another god,
Cried out 'God bless us,' but that was before she saw
The white foam breaking through her lips and her rolling
The pupils of her eyes and her face all bloodless.
Then she raised a different cry from that 'God bless us,'
A huge shriek, and the women ran, one to the king,
One to the newly wedded husband to tell him
What had happened to his bride; and with frequent sound
The whole of the palace rang as they went running.
One walking quickly round the course of a race-track
Would now have turned the bend and be close to the goal,
When she, poor girl, opened her shut and speechless eye,
And with a terrible groan she came to herself.
For a two-fold pain was moving up against her.
The wreath of gold that was resting around her head
Let forth a fearful stream of all-devouring fire,
And the finely-woven dress your children gave to her,
Was fastening on the unhappy girl's fine flesh.
She leapt up from the chair, and all on fire she ran,
Shaking her hair now this way and now that, trying
To hurl the diadem away; but fixedly
The gold preserved its grip, and, when she shook her hair,
Then more and twice as fiercely the fire blazed out.
Till, beaten by her fate, she fell down to the ground,
Hard to be recognised except by a parent.
Neither the setting of her eyes was plain to see,
Nor the shapeliness of her face. From the top of
Her head there oozed out blood and fire mixed together.
Like the drops on pine-bark, so the flesh from her bones
Dropped away, torn by the hidden fang of the poison.
It was a fearful sight; and terror held us all
From touching the corpse. We had learned from what
    had happened.

But her wretched father, knowing nothing of the event,
Came suddenly to the house, and fell upon the corpse,
And at once cried out and folded his arms about her,
And kissed her and spoke to her, saying 'O my poor child,
What heavenly power has so shamefully destroyed you?
And who has set me here like an ancient sepulchre,
Deprived of you? O let me die with you, my child!'
And when he had made an end of his wailing and crying,
Then the old man wished to raise himself to his feet;
But, as the ivy clings to the twigs of the laurel,
So he stuck to the fine dress, and he struggled fearfully.
For he was trying to lift himself to his knee,
And she was pulling him down, and when he tugged hard
He would be ripping his aged flesh from his bones.
At last his life was quenched and the unhappy man
Gave up the ghost, no longer could hold up his head.
There they lie close, the daughter and the old father,
Dead bodies, an event he prayed for in his tears.
As for your interests, I will say nothing of them,
For you will find your own escape from punishment.
Our human life I think and have thought a shadow,
And I do not fear to say that those who are held
Wise amongst men and who search the reasons of things
Are those who bring the most sorrow on themselves.
For of mortals there is no one who is happy.
If wealth flows in upon one, one may be perhaps
Luckier than one's neighbour, but still not happy.

                                                    [*Exit.*]

CHORUS

Heaven, it seems, on this day has fastened many
Evils on Jason, and Jason has deserved them.
Poor girl, the daughter of Kreon, how I pity you
And your misfortunes, you who have gone quite away
To the house of Hades because of marrying Jason.

MEDEA

Women, my task is fixed: as quickly as I may
To kill my children, and start away from this land,
And not, by wasting time, to suffer my children
To be slain by another hand less kindly to them.
Force every way will have it they must die, and since

64

This must be so, then I, their mother, shall kill them.
O arm yourself in steel, my heart! Do not hang back
From doing this fearful and necessary wrong.
O come, my hand, poor wretched hand, and take the
    sword,
Take it, step forward to this bitter starting point,
And do not be a coward, do not think of them,
How sweet they are, and how you are their mother. Just for
This one short day be forgetful of your children,
Afterwards weep; for even though you will kill them,
They were very dear,—O, I am an unhappy woman!

[*With a cry she rushes into the house.*]

### CHORUS

O Earth, and the far shining
Ray of the Sun, look down, look down upon
This poor lost woman, look, before she raises
The hand of murder against her flesh and blood.
Yours was the golden birth from which
She sprang, and now I fear divine
Blood may be shed by men.
O heavenly light, hold back her hand,
Check her, and drive from out the house
The bloody Fury raised by fiends of Hell.

Vain waste, your care of children;
Was it in vain you bore the babes you loved,
After you passed the inhospitable strait
Between the dark blue rocks, Symplegades?
O wretched one, how has it come,
This heavy anger on your heart,
This cruel bloody mind?
For God from mortals asks a stern
Price for the stain of kindred blood
In like disaster falling on their homes.

[*A cry from one of the children is heard.*]

### CHORUS

Do you hear the cry, do you hear the children's cry?
O you hard heart, O woman fated for evil

ONE OF THE CHILDREN [*from within*]
What can I do and how escape my mother's hands?

ANOTHER CHILD [*from within*]
O my dear brother, I cannot tell. We are lost.

CHORUS
Shall I enter the house? O surely I should
Defend the children from murder.

A CHILD [*from within*]
O help us, in God's name, for now we need your help.
Now, now we are close to it. We are trapped by the sword.

CHORUS
O your heart must have been made of rock or steel,
You who can kill
With your own hand the fruit of your own womb.
Of one alone I have heard, one woman alone
Of those of old who laid her hands on her children,
Ino, sent mad by heaven when the wife of Zeus
Drove her out from her home and made her wander;
And because of the wicked shedding of blood
Of her own children she threw
Herself, poor wretch, into the sea and stepped away
Over the sea-cliff to die with her two children.
What horror more can be? O women's love,
So full of trouble,
How many evils have you caused already!

[*Enter Jason, with attendants.*]

JASON
You women, standing close in front of this dwelling,
Is she, Medea, she who did this dreadful deed,
Still in the house, or has she run away in flight?
For she will have to hide herself beneath the earth,
Or raise herself on wings into the height of air,
If she wishes to escape the royal vengeance.
Does she imagine that, having killed our rulers,
She will herself escape uninjured from this house?
But I am thinking not so much of her as for
The children,—her the king's friends will make to suffer
For what she did. So I have come to save the lives

66

Of my boys, in case the royal house should harm them
While taking vengeance for their mother's wicked deed.

CHORUS

O Jason, if you but knew how deeply you are
Involved in sorrow, you would not have spoken so.

JASON

What is it? That she is planning to kill me also?

CHORUS

Your children are dead, and by their own mother's hand.

JASON

What! This is it? O woman, you have destroyed me.

CHORUS

You must make up your mind your children are no more.

JASON

Where did she kill them? Was it here or in the house?

CHORUS

Open the gates and there you will see them murdered.

JASON

Quick as you can unlock the doors, men, and undo
The fastenings and let me see this double evil,
My children dead and her,—O her I will repay.

[*His attendants rush to the door. Medea appears
above the house in a chariot drawn by dragons.
She has the dead bodies of the children with her.*]

MEDEA

Why do you batter these gates and try to unbar them,
Seeking the corpses and for me who did the deed?
You may cease your trouble, and, if you have need of me,
Speak, if you wish. You will never touch me with your
      hand,
Such a chariot has Helios, my father's father,
Given me to defend me from my enemies.

JASON

You hateful thing, you woman most utterly loathed
By the gods and me and by all the race of mankind,
You who have had the heart to raise a sword against
Your children, you, their mother, and left me childless,—

67

You have done this, and do you still look at the sun
And at the earth, after these most fearful doings?
I wish you dead. Now I see it plain, though at that time
I did not, when I took you from your foreign home
And brought you to a Greek house, you, an evil thing,
A traitress to your father and your native land.
The gods hurled the avenging curse of yours on me.
For your own brother you slew at your own hearthside,
And then came aboard that beautiful ship, the Argo.
And that was your beginning. When you were married
To me, your husband, and had borne children to me,
For the sake of pleasure in the bed you killed them.
There is no Greek woman who would have dared such
      deeds,
Out of all those whom I passed over and chose you
To marry instead, a bitter destructive match,
A monster not a woman, having a nature
Wilder than that of Scylla in the Tuscan sea.
Ah! no, not if I had ten thousand words of shame
Could I sting you. You are naturally so brazen.
Go, worker in evil, stained with your children's blood.
For me remains to cry aloud upon my fate,
Who will get no pleasure from my newly-wedded love,
And the boys whom I begot and brought up, never
Shall I speak to them alive. Oh, my life is over!

MEDEA

Long would be the answer which I might have made to
These words of yours, if Zeus the father did not know
How I have treated you and what you did to me.
No, it was not to be that you should scorn my love,
And pleasantly live your life through, laughing at me;
Nor would the princess, nor he who offered the match,
Kreon, drive me away without paying for it.
So now you may call me a monster, if you wish,
O Scylla housed in the caves of the Tuscan sea
I too, as I had to, have taken hold of your heart.

JASON

You feel the pain yourself. You share in my sorrow.

MEDEA

Yes, and my grief is gain when you cannot mock it.

68

**JASON**

O children, what a wicked mother she was to you!

**MEDEA**

They died from a disease they caught from their father.

**JASON**

I tell you it was not my hand that destroyed them.

**MEDEA**

But it was your insolence, and your virgin wedding.

**JASON**

And just for the sake of that you chose to kill them.

**MEDEA**

Is love so small a pain, do you think, for a woman?

**JASON**

For a wise one, certainly. But you are wholly evil.

**MEDEA**

The children are dead. I say this to make you suffer.

**JASON**

The children, I think, will bring down curses on you.

**MEDEA**

The gods know who was the author of this sorrow.

**JASON**

Yes, the gods know indeed, they know your loathsome
heart.

**MEDEA**

Hate me. But I tire of your barking bitterness.

**JASON**

And I of yours. It is easier to leave you.

**MEDEA**

How then? What shall I do? I long to leave you too.

**JASON**

Give me the bodies to bury and to mourn them.

**MEDEA**

No, that I will not. I will bury them myself,

Bearing them to Hera's temple on the promontory;
So that no enemy may evilly treat them
By tearing up their grave. In this land of Corinth
I shall establish a holy feast and sacrifice
Each year for ever to atone for the blood guilt.
And I myself go to the land of Erechtheus
To dwell in Aigeus' house, the son of Pandion.
While you, as is right, will die without distinction,
Struck on the head by a piece of the Argo's timber,
And you will have seen the bitter end of my love.

JASON

May a Fury for the children's sake destroy you,
And justice. Requiter of blood.

MEDEA

What heavenly power lends an ear
To a breaker of oaths, a deceiver?

JASON

O, I hate you, murderess of children.

MEDEA

Go to your palace. Bury your bride.

JASON

I go, with two children to mourn for.

MEDEA

Not yet do you feel it. Wait for the future.

JASON

Oh, children I loved!

MEDEA

I loved them, you did not.

JASON

You loved them, and killed them.

MEDEA

To make you feel pain.

JASON

Oh, wretch that I am, how I long
To kiss the dear lips of my children!

70

#### MEDEA

Now you would speak to them, now you would kiss them.
Then you rejected them.

#### JASON

Let me, I beg you,
Touch my boys' delicate flesh.

#### MEDEA

I will not. Your words are all wasted.

#### JASON

O God, do you hear it, this persecution,
These my sufferings from this hateful
Woman, this monster, murderess of children?
Still what I can do that I will do:
I will lament and cry upon heaven,
Calling the gods to bear me witness
How you have killed my boys and prevent me from
Touching their bodies or giving them burial.
I wish I had never begot them to see them
Afterwards slaughtered by you.

#### CHORUS

Zeus in Olympus is the overseer
Of many doings. Many things the gods
Achieve beyond our judgement. What we thought
Is not confirmed and what we thought not God
Contrives. And so it happens in this story.

# The HIPPOLYTUS
of
# EURIPIDES

# THE CHARACTERS

THESEUS, *king of Athens*
HIPPOLYTUS, *his son*
PHAEDRA, *wife of Theseus*
APHRODITE } *two rival goddesses*
ARTEMIS
ATTENDANT *to Hippolytus*
NURSE *to Phaedra*
SERVANT
MESSENGER
CHORUS OF THE WOMEN OF TROEZEN
ATTENDANTS

# Introduction

ALTHOUGH THE MAIN elements of the plot of *Hippolytus* are set out in the first speech, or prologue, some knowledge of the background of the characters is still valuable for the understanding of the play.

Theseus, king of Athens, was the son, according to some legends, of Aigeus, according to others, of Poseidon, the god of the sea. Among his many exploits in youth was the carrying off of Antiope, sister of the Queen of the Amazons. Hippolytus was the son of Theseus and Antiope. He was brought up in Troezen by Pittheus, father of Theseus' mother Aethra.

Later Theseus married Phaedra, daughter of Minos, king of Crete. The family, apart from Minos himself, was notorious for extravagant or unhappy love affairs. Phaedra's mother was Pasiphae who, after her passion for the bull, gave birth to the Minotaur which was finally killed by Theseus. Her sister was Ariadne who, after falling in love with Theseus, and being deserted by him, was carried away by Dionysus. By Phaedra Theseus had two sons who, in the play, are alluded to as 'true-born,' Hippolytus himself being regarded as illegitimate.

Hippolytus, as is clear from his first appearance in the play, is the devoted worshipper of the virgin goddess Artemis. He is even privileged to hear her voice and feel her presence while he is hunting. Wholly devoted to her, he has no time or inclination for the rival and opposite deity, Aphrodite, who decides to revenge herself on him for his neglect of her. The means she chooses are to make Phaedra fall in love with him, and to present Theseus with a false picture of what has happened, so that he will call down on Hippolytus one of the curses which his father Poseidon has empowered him to make. Hippolytus will be killed and Phaedra, though entirely innocent, will, in order to involve Hippolytus in ruin, take her own life.

On the face of it such a story might seem to be an

attack on 'the ways of God to men' of the kind which Euripides does make sometimes, though not nearly so often as is commonly thought. He has been called a rationalist and a free-thinker, and in a sense the descriptions are justified. But his 'rationalism' is not in the least like Shaw's and his 'free thought' is always conscious of the wider boundaries of the poetic imagination.

In this play it is quite true that the attitude of Aphrodite, if we regard her as a real person, must appear as mean, savage, unscrupulous—anything but divine. There seems also to be a manifest inefficiency in the divine ordering of things when we discover that Artemis, a goddess of equal power with Aphrodite, can do nothing to preserve her innocent and trusting favourite—nothing except promise that in the end, by causing the death of Adonis, she will get even with her rival. Yet it must not be assumed that, because, by human standards, the gods in this play behave badly, therefore Euripides was writing irreligiously or with any notion of 'debunking' popular belief.

His purpose is certainly a wider one than this, and his goddesses are used as symbols to define and circumscribe a human problem. The problem is a familiar one in Greek tragedy. It is of the dangers involved in any kind of self-security or pride, and of the existence of powers which are more effective and perhaps, in the last resort, higher than justice. Hippolytus, like Prometheus, is innocent; yet, in his intense concentration on one aspect of reality, he is also guilty. It is not quite that he is too good, but that, by failing to appreciate other forces which exist, he sins by pride. His own virgin ideals may certainly seem higher ones than are the wholly physical and emotional claims which are made for love in the play. But the point is that Hippolytus will not even admit that such things exist. Though by no stretch of imagination can he be said to have deserved his fate, yet his fate is an example of something which happens. It is a heroic fate and the audience who saw the play performed in Athens in the year 428 B.C. would be aware that across the water in Troezen Hippolytus was still worshipped as a hero, and that in front of his tomb girls still before their marriage made offerings of the tresses of their hair.

It is interesting to recall that out of Euripides' seventy-five plays this was one of the five that received a first prize at the Athenian dramatic festival. It was produced just after the great plague of Athens in which, among many others, Pericles lost his life. The very last lines of the play are held, with some reason, to have been taken by the audience as a reference to this great statesman's death.

# The HIPPOLYTUS of EURIPIDES

*[The scene is in Troezen, in front of the palace of King Theseus. By the gates are two statues, one of Aphrodite and one of Artemis. The goddess Aphrodite speaks.]*

### APHRODITE

STRONG am I among mortals, not without a name,
the goddess Cypris, who in heaven too is known.
And of those who live and look upon the light of the sun
from Pontus to the boundaries that Atlas set,
I give honour to the ones who reverence my power,
and those whose thoughts of me are arrogant I crush.
You will find this holds even among the gods above:
they too are pleased when they receive the praise of men.
And I will show at once that what I say is true.
The son of Theseus from the Amazon his wife,
Hippolytus, brought up by Pittheus, that saintly man,
alone of all the people in this land, Troezen,
considers me the least important of the gods,
spurns love making and will not join in an embrace.
Instead he worships Phoebus' sister, Artemis,
the child of Zeus, and thinks her greatest of the gods,
and always with the virgin goddess in green woods
he clears the land of beasts with his swift hunting dogs,
in mightier company than that of human kind.
All this I do not grudge him. Why indeed should I?
But for sinning against me, upon this very day
I shall take vengeance on Hippolytus. The work
is begun already; there is not much left to do.
For once he came to Athens from the house of Pittheus
to see and to receive the holy mysteries,
and then his father's noble and respected wife,
Phaedra, first saw him, and she found her heart in the
     grip
of savage passion. This was as I planned it for her.
And before she came into this land of Troezen,

she built upon the rock of Pallas, looking out
over this land, a temple to me, the Cyprian.
Her love was absent, but it was for him she made
the temple and afterwards she called it by his name.
And now that Theseus, fleeing from the stain of blood
of Pallas' murdered sons, has taken on himself
one year of foreign exile and has left the land
of Cecrops and has sailed to this land with his wife,
now she, poor woman, wastes away in agony,
and, driven from her senses by the stings of love,
suffers in silence. No one with her knows her pain.
But this is not the way this love of hers must end.
I shall let Theseus know of it. All will come out.
Then this young man, my enemy, will be destroyed
by the curses of his father; for the lord of the sea,
Poseidon, gave to Theseus as an honoured right
that he should pray three times and have his prayer ful-
    filled.
As for the woman, Phaedra, she shall keep her name,
but none the less shall die. I shall not think her pain
of enough importance to prevent my enemies
from suffering the punishment that I think fit.
But now I see the son of Theseus coming here,
Hippolytus, fresh from his hunting exercise.
I therefore shall be gone. Behind him comes a great
and merry band of hunters, singing to Artemis,
hymning the goddess's praise. He does not know the gates
of Hell are open and this day he sees his last.

[*Aphrodite goes out. Hippolytus, carrying a
garland in his hand, enters followed by his attendants.*]

HIPPOLYTUS
Sing, as you follow me, sing of her
    heavenly daughter of Zeus,
Artemis, in whose care we are.

ATTENDANTS [*singing*]
Most holy lady, we worship you,
    child of the Highest.
We worship you, Lady Artemis,
Leto and Zeus's daughter.

79

You most beautiful far among
    maidens, you who in heaven dwell
    in the space of your father's court,
    in the golden palace of Zeus,
    hear us, most beautiful
    maid among maidens in heaven, most
    beautiful, Artemis.

[*Hippolytus advances to the statue of Artemis
in front of the palace.*]

### HIPPOLYTUS

For you, my lady, I have made and bring to you
this wreath of twined flowers from a virgin meadow,
a place where never shepherd thought to feed his flocks
nor ever came the stroke of iron. Instead the bees
cross and recross this virgin meadow in the spring.
And native Shame waters the ground with river dew,
and from his garden only those may pluck the flowers
who were elect from birth by a wise purity
in all things, and never had to learn it. Evil men
have no right there. And so, dear lady, take from this
reverent hand a binding for your golden hair.
For I alone of men am so distinguished as to be
constantly with you and to speak and hear your words.
I hear the voice, but I have never seen your face.
O, let me end my life as I have started it!

[*One of his attendants approaches him.*]

### ATTENDANT

Sir, for 'master' is a word I use for gods—
if I gave good advice, would you receive it from me?

### HIPPOLYTUS

Of course I would. It would be stupid not to do so.

### ATTENDANT

Do you know of a rule that is general among men?

### HIPPOLYTUS

What rule? What is it you are telling me about?

### ATTENDANT

People hate pride and an exclusive attitude.

80

**HIPPOLYTUS**

Quite right. An arrogant person is always hated.

**ATTENDANT**

And people are grateful when you talk to them kindly.

**HIPPOLYTUS**

Certainly. It does much good, and costs little trouble.

**ATTENDANT**

And do you think that the same thing is true of gods?

**HIPPOLYTUS**

Yes, since we mortals live by the same rules as they.

**ATTENDANT**

Then why do you not say a word to a great goddess?

**HIPPOLYTUS**

Which one? Be careful that you name what can be
named.

**ATTENDANT**

The one that stands there. The Cyprian at your gates.

**HIPPOLYTUS**

Since I live cleanly, I greet her from a distance.

**ATTENDANT**

Yet she is great and proud and known among all men.

**HIPPOLYTUS**

I do not care for gods men worship in the night.

**ATTENDANT**

Still you must recognise the honours due to gods.

**HIPPOLYTUS**

Both among gods and men there are different tastes.

**ATTENDANT**

Then I wish you happiness, and the sense you ought to
have.

**HIPPOLYTUS** [*turning away from him*]

Come on, my friends, and go inside the house and see
the banquet is prepared. After a day of hunting
a well-spread table does one good. Let someone rub
the horses down. When I have had enough to eat,
I shall yoke and drive them out today for exercise.

As for your Cyprian goddess—may she be in luck.
   [*He goes into the palace. The Attendant remains
   behind and bows before the statue of Aphrodite.*]

But I (and here I shall not imitate young men)
think in a way a slave should think before he speaks.
Let me address my prayers to your holy image,
goddess of Cyprus. You should have some pity on
one who, because of his youth, with violent feelings
speaks nonsense of you. You should pretend not to hear.
Gods should be wiser and more moderate than men.

   [*He follows the others into the palace. Enter the
   Chorus of Women of Troezen.*]

CHORUS
There is a rock that wells with Ocean's water
and from its steeps lets fall a flowing stream
where pitchers . dip, and there
one that I knew was plunging
red robes in the river dew,
spreading the robes to dry on the slab of a hot
rock in the sun, and she
told me first of the queen.

How she is wasting on a bed of sickness
inside her house, and hides her golden head
in the shade of a silken veil;
and now for the third day she
refrains with her lovely lips
from the touch of the grains of Demaeter, and secretly
suffering, longs to draw in
to the pitiful harbour of death.

Are you astray, my lady,
possessed by a god—by Pan
or Hecate or the terrible
Corybantes, or Mountain Mother?
Or are you wasted away for a sin incurred
by failing, unsanctified, to sacrifice

to the goddess of beasts, Dictynna?
For she is able to range through the waves
over the ocean to land
on the salt and eddying waters.

Is it your husband, the noble
king of Erechtheus' sons?
Is he folded in secret love
away from your bed in the house?
Or has some mariner sailed from the port of Crete
to this most kindly harbour for sailing men
and brought to our queen a message?
And is it in grief for what she has learnt
of suffering there in her home
that she lies heartsick in her bed?

In women's difficult unstable natures
a pitiful helplessness often dwells
springing from pangs in the womb and unbalanced
    thought.
Such an impulse of pain
through my loins also has darted, but then I cried
to heavenly Artemis, giver of gentle birth,
goddess guarding the bow, and she for ever
is honoured and blessed by me as she goes with the gods.

    [*Enter Phaedra and her old Nurse. Phaedra lies
    down on a couch.*]

But here at the door is the aged nurse
bringing her mistress out of the palace.
The lowering cloud on her brows is darker.
What can it be? I long to discover
what can have happened
so to alter the form of the queen.

NURSE

How people suffer! How hateful is illness!
What shall I do for you? What leave undone?
Here is the light for you, here is the bright sky.
Here is your sickbed ready for you
outside your doors.
What you wanted was always to come here,

83

though soon you will hurry back to your bedroom,
soon disappointed. Nothing can please you.
Discontented with what you have, you
think what you don't have is better.
I would rather be ill than look after an illness.
Illness is simple, but nursing an illness brings
grief to the heart and work for the hands.
The life of men is nothing but evil,
nor is there any respite from suffering.
Yet if there is a state better than living,
darkness surrounds it and hides it in clouds.
So we show ourselves lovesick indeed
for this something that glitters on earth,
having no knowledge of different living
and no revelation of what is beneath,
since there's no direction in idle legends.

### PHAEDRA

Lift me upright, give support to my head.
Dear women, the bonds of my limbs are unloosed.
Take hold of my hands and my delicate arms.
Heavy to wear is the veil on my head.
Take it, and let my hair loose on my shoulders.

### NURSE

Be patient, my child, and do not so fiercely
toss to and fro.
If you keep quiet and are brave in your spirit,
you will find your illness more easy to bear.
It is fated for mortals to suffer.

### PHAEDRA

Alas! how I wish I could draw from a dewy
fountain a draught of the shining waters,
and take my rest in a leafy meadow,
lying beneath the shade of the poplars.

### NURSE

O my child, what is this you are saying?
Really, you must not before all these people
speak and let loose such words ridden by madness.

Away to the mountains! I will go to the wild wood,
under the pines, where the hounds are hunting,
and pressing their chase on the dappled deer.
O, let me do it! I long to be shouting
out to the hounds, and to poise by my yellow
hair the Thessalian javelin, and carry
the bladed lance in my hand.

**NURSE**

My child, why ever should such things upset you?
Why should you take such an interest in hunting?
Why should you long for a draught from a fountain?
Here, close by your towers, is a dewy slope,
and from here we can fetch you some water.

**PHAEDRA**

Artemis, queen of sea-girt Limne,
queen of the race-course that echoes with hoof-beats,
O how I long to be there in your lowlands,
breaking in the Venetian horses!

**NURSE**

What are these words that you fling out in madness?
Only just now you were off to the mountains,
led by a longing for hunting, and now you
yearn for horses on sandy plains
away from the sea. It would take some divining
to find, my child, which one of the gods
holds the reins of your spirit, and drives it astray.

**PHAEDRA**

What can I have done to make me unhappy?
And whither so driven aside from my right mind?
I am mad, I have fallen through spite of some god,
O, poor wretch that I am.
Cover my face again, dear mother.
I feel dread at the words I have spoken.
Cover it up. Tears start in my eyes,
and shame has come over my face.
To come to my senses again is an agony;
yet this madness is evil. The best thing of all

is to die, and not know what I'm doing.

There, I've covered your face. But, O when will my body
be shrouded in death?
Much I have learned by living a long time.
Mortals, I know, should join with each other
in loving feelings that are not excessive,
just on the surface, not touching the quick of the soul.
Light should the heart's affections lie on us,
quick to cast off and quick to pull tighter.
This is a heavy weight, that one soul
should suffer itself for two souls,
just as I for my mistress grieve too greatly.
In life, they say, one finds more failure
than delight in this unswerving
heart's devotion, which conflicts with health.
'Nothing in excess' is better
far than counsels of perfection.
Wise men will agree with me.

CHORUS

You aged woman, trusted nurse to this our queen.
We see the unhappy sufferings that Phaedra feels,
but what the illness is is still unknown to us.
From you we wish to hear and be informed of it.

NURSE

I have asked and do not know. She does not wish to
speak.

CHORUS

Nor what was the beginning of these pains of hers?

NURSE

Just the same thing. On all of this she is silent.

CHORUS

How weak she is, and how her body wastes away!

NURSE

No wonder, since for three days she has touched no food.

CHORUS

Is it some curse of god or that she aims to die?

NURSE

She wants to die, and starves to make an end of life.

CHORUS

It is a strange thing if her husband bears this calmly.

NURSE

She hides her pains from him and says she is not ill.

CHORUS

But when he sees her face, does he not see she is?

NURSE

No. Just now he happens to be away from home.

CHORUS

Can you not try and force some way of finding out
what is her illness and what distraction of her mind?

NURSE

I have tried everything and met with no success.
But even now I'll not relax my efforts for her,
so that you too, being here, may bear me witness
how true I am to a mistress in her misfortune.

[*She turns to Phaedra.*]

Come, my dear child, and let us both forget those words
we spoke before. You must behave with more kindness,
relax that angry frown and change your way of mind;
and I, if in any way I failed to understand,
will let that be, and turn to other better words.
Now, if your illness is the kind that one keeps private,
here are these women ready to assist you in it.
But if your suffering can be disclosed to men,
speak, so that we can let the doctors know of it.
Now, come! Why don't you speak? You ought to tell me,
   child.
If what I say is not right, point it out to me;
otherwise you should agree with my well-meant advice.
Say something, do. Or look at me.—Poor wretch I am!
Women, it does no good, the trouble that we take.
We are still as far away as ever. The last time
words could not soften her, and now she will not hear.

[*She turns to Phaedra again.*]

Yet listen to this. Now, if you like, be more self-willed
than is the sea itself. Dying, you will betray
your children, leaving them without their share in all

87

their father's wealth. Yes, she, the Amazon huntress,
the royal lady, bore a master for your sons,
a bastard aiming at full rights. You know him well.
Hippolytus.

PHAEDRA

Alas!

NURSE

What! This point touches you?

PHAEDRA

Mother, you have destroyed me. Please, I beg of you,
never again make mention of this man to me.

NURSE

You see? Your mind is sound, and yet in spite of that
you will not help your children and preserve your life.

PHAEDRA

I love my children. Other evils storm my heart.

NURSE

Are your hands pure, my child, from stain of shedding
blood?

PHAEDRA

My hands are pure: it is my mind that has the stain.

NURSE

Some enemy brings pain on you by magic means.

PHAEDRA

Against his will and mine a friend is killing me.

NURSE

Is it Theseus who has done some injury to you?

PHAEDRA

Let me be never found to have done him a wrong!

NURSE

What is this fearful thing that drives you on to death?

PHAEDRA

Leave me to sin. It is not against you I sin.

NURSE

I'll never leave you. It is your fault if I fail.

[*She throws herself on her knees in front of Phaedra.*]

PHAEDRA

What are you doing, clinging to my hands and forcing me?

NURSE

Yes, and I clasp your knees and will not let you go.

PHAEDRA

Poor thing, my words are bad for you to hear, yes, bad.

NURSE

Could anything be worse for me than to lose you?

PHAEDRA

You will be lost. And yet to me this thing gives fame.

NURSE

Yet you hide something good, in spite of all my prayers?

PHAEDRA

Yes, since the glory that I plan proceeds from shame.

NURSE

Then you will be more honoured still by telling it.

PHAEDRA

Leave me, I beg you, and let go of my right hand.

NURSE

Never! You will not give me what you ought to give.

PHAEDRA

I will. For I respect your rights in pleading so.

NURSE

Then I'll be silent. Now it is for you to speak.

PHAEDRA

O my mother, what a love, poor thing, you fell into!

NURSE

Is what you mean, my child, her passion for the bull?

PHAEDRA

You too, my wretched sister, Dionysus' wife.

NURSE

What is it, child? You speak ill of your family.

**PHAEDRA**

And I, the third unhappy one, I too destroyed!

**NURSE**

I am indeed bewildered. Where will these words end?

**PHAEDRA**

Where I became unhappy, a long time ago.

**NURSE**

But still I know no more of what I wish to hear.

**PHAEDRA**

Ah!
I wish that you could say the words I have to say.

**NURSE**

I am no prophetess to make the dark things clear.

**PHAEDRA**

What do they mean when they say people are in love?

**NURSE**

Something most sweet, my child, and also painful too.

**PHAEDRA**

I must be one who feels the painfulness of it.

**NURSE**

What's this you say? You are in love, my child?
With whom?

**PHAEDRA**

There is a man I know, the son of the Amazon . . .

**NURSE**

Hippolytus?

**PHAEDRA**

You heard it from your lips, not mine.

**NURSE**

Ah, child, what can you mean? O, you have ruined me.
Women, this is not to be borne, and I will not
bear to live more. Ill day, ill light it is I see.
I shall throw and cast away my body, leave my life
and die. I say farewell, since I no longer am.
Against their will, perhaps, but all the same, the wise
and chaste love evil. Cypris, then, is not divine,

but must be something else more mighty than a god
to have destroyed my mistress, me, and all our house.

Oh, did you hear her? Oh, did you listen
to things unutterable, to the queen
as she told her woes?
O let me die, dear lady, before
I come to a mind like yours! Oh alas!
O poor wretch in your pains!
O troubles in which men live!
You are destroyed, you have brought bad things to the
    light.
What waits for you now through this long day?
Some new evil will fall on this house.
No longer doubtful the destination
of Cypris' will, O unhappy daughter of Crete.

You women of Troezen, you who live here upon
this verge and entrance to the country of Pelops,
before now idly in the watches of the night
I have considered how the life of man is spoilt.
And to my mind it is not through a lack of wit
that men go wrong, since, as for being sensible,
many are that. But this is how I look at it:
we understand and recognise what things are good,
but do not do them, some because of laziness,
others by choosing pleasure of some kind instead
of honour. There are many pleasures in our life,—
long conversations, being idle (a delightful fault),
and shame. There are two kinds of shame,—the one not bad
the other a weight on houses. If they were marked out
clearly, the two would not be spelt in the same way
Now, since it happens that I think as I have said,
the medicine does not exist by which I was
likely to change and fall back from this view of mine.
Now to you too I shall describe my way of thought.
When passion wounded me, I tried to find the way
by which I could bear it with most honour. I began
in this way,—to keep silent and conceal my pain.
There is no trusting in the tongue, which well enough

91

knows how to criticise the thoughts of other men,
yet on its own self oftenest brings suffering.
And then my second resolution was to bear
my folly nobly and by reason conquer it.
And, as a third resource, since by these means I failed
to subdue Cypris, I made up my mind to die;
and this (no one will question it) is the best plan.
For I would never wish my good deeds to be hid,
nor to have people watching me when I do ill.
The deed, I knew, was shameful and my own disease;
clearly I knew as well that I was a woman,
something that's loathed by all. My curses on the wife
who first began, by taking lovers, to bring shame
upon the marriage bed! It was from noble houses
this evil started to descend on womankind.
When what is shameful is condoned by noble people,
then certainly the lower class will think it good.
And then I hate the women who in words are chaste,
while hiding secretly their bold dishonest deeds.
O sea-born lady Cypris, how can these ones ever
look in the faces of their husbands and not fear
and tremble lest the darkness that has covered them
and rooms within their houses might not cry aloud?
This is the thing, my friends, that drives me to my death:
lest I be found to have brought shame on my husband
and on the children whom I bore. I want them free
to live and free to speak and prosperous to dwell
in glorious Athens, famous for their mother's sake.
Consciousness of a father's or a mother's sins
enslaves a man, however stout his heart may be.
And this alone, they say, to those who have it, can
be matched with life itself,—a good and upright mind.
Time, at some moment, must bring evil men to light,
holding to them, as to the face of some young girl,
a mirror up. May I be never seen with them!

CHORUS

Ah, how what's wise and chaste is honoured everywhere,
and among men it bears the fruit of good report!

NURSE

My mistress, as you saw, just now the news of your

predicament filled me with sudden dreadful fear.
But now I think that I was silly. Among men
one's second thoughts are in a way the wiser ones.
To you nothing outrageous or unheard-of has
happened. It is the goddess' anger strikes at you.
You are in love. What's strange in that? Most people are.
And then because of love will you destroy your life?
There'll be no point in loving those who are close to us
now or in future, if one has to die for it.
Cypris is irresistible when in full force,
but gently visits those whose spirits yield to her;
and when she finds a man who's proud and arrogant,
of course she seizes him and makes a mock of him.
She ranges through the air, and in the surge of sea
there Cypris is, and everything proceeds from her.
And she it is who plants in us and gives desire
from which all we inhabitants of earth are born.
Indeed those people who possess the books of old
writers and are themselves great readers of their works
know how Zeus once desired to have the joys of love
with Semele, and know how once fair-shining Dawn
snatched up to heaven Cephalus to join the gods,
and all this out of passion; and yet, all the same,
they dwell in heaven, do not shun the paths of gods,
and are, I think, quite pleased to yield to what has passed.
Will you object? Your father then should have made you
on special terms, or else controlled by other gods,
if you will not consent to follow these known laws.
How many men, and wise ones, are there, do you think,
who see their beds defiled, and pretend not to see?
How many fathers who assist their erring sons
in finding love affairs? Amongst the wise this is
a general rule,—to hide what is not fair to see.
Nor should men try to be too strict about their lives.
They cannot even make the roofs, with which their homes
are covered, absolutely right. And you, fallen
to such a state, how can you hope to swim out clear?
No, if the good in you is greater than the bad,
you, being only human, will do very well.
So, please, my dear child, give up these bad thoughts
    of yours.

Give up your arrogance, for it is nothing else
but arrogance to wish to have more strength than gods.
Love, and be bold. It is a god that willed all this.
You may be ill, but find a way to come out well.
Charms do exist and words that soothe and sway the mind.
We shall discover medicine for this ill of yours.
Indeed it's true that men would still be looking for it,
unless it was we women could find out the way.

Phaedra, she tells you things that are more useful to you
in your present distress. Yet I think *you* are right.
And you will find this view of mine more hard to bear
than are her words, more painful too to listen to.

This is the thing that ruins the well-ordered towns
and homes of men,—words spoken too persuasively.
For people should not say what charms the listener's ear
but what will bring to those who hear it good report.

Why this grand language? What you need is not fine
    words
but to find out as fast as possible about
the man, and us to tell him the straight story of you.
For if it was not that your life was in this state
of peril, if you were a woman more controlled,
I never would, because of love and your delights,
have urged you on so far; but now the struggle is
to save your life, and I cannot be blamed for this.

What awful things you say! Will you please keep your
    mouth
shut, and never again speak such disgraceful words.

Disgraceful, yes, but better for you than your fine
words, and a better deed if I can save your life
than save your name, to glory in which name you'd die.

Please, not to me, I beg you (you speak well, but foully)
go any further now. My heart is well prepared

by love, and, if you speak so well of shameful things,
I shall be swept away by what I fly from now.

NURSE

If this is what you think, you ought not to have sinned.
You have. Then listen to me, for the next best thing
is to give way. I have at home some soothing draughts
for love,—the thought has only just occurred to me,—
and these, without dishonour, doing no harm to your wits,
will free you from your sickness, if you will be brave.
But I must have something from him whom you desire,
some mark, either a lock of hair or piece of clothing,
so from the two of you to make consentment one.

PHAEDRA

Is this a drug to drink or ointment to put on?

NURSE

I do not know. Be happy and never mind, my child.

PHAEDRA

I am afraid that you may be too clever in all this.

NURSE

Be sure you would fear everything. What do you fear?

PHAEDRA

That you might tell some word of this to Theseus' son.

NURSE

Leave me alone, my child. I shall arrange things well.
   [*She turns to go into the palace but first ad-
   dresses the statue of Aphrodite.*]
Only be you my helper, lady of the sea,
Cypris! As for what else I have within my mind
it will be enough to tell it to our friends indoors.
                    [*She goes into the palace.*]

CHORUS

Love, O Love, you that make well to the eyes
drops of desire, you that bring sweet delight
into the hearts that you with your force invade,
never to me appear in catastrophe,
never in discord come!
Since there exists no bolt of the fire and no

95

weightier bolt of the stars than that
arrow of Aphrodite hurled
out of the hands of Love,
Love, the child of the Highest.

Useless it is that still by Alpheus' stream,
Useless it is by Phoebus's Pythian shrines
for the land of Hellas to sacrifice more and more
blood of oxen, when we neglect to give
the honour that's due to Love,
Love, the ruler of men, he who keeps the keys
of Aphrodite's pleasantest dwelling-place,
he who ravages on his way,
bringing to mortals all
catastrophes at his coming.

The girl in Oichalia,
a maiden unyoked to love,
unmarried as yet and husbandless, Cypris took
and loosed her from home in ships,
and, a fugitive thing, like a nymph or Bacchante, she
    gave her,
with blood and with fire
and murder for wedding hymns,
to Alcmene's child.
Poor wretch she was in her marriage!

O holy fortress of Thebes,
O fountain of Dirce, you
well could witness the force of Cypris' coming.
For with thunder and lightning flash
she brought to her bed the mother of Bacchus, the Zeus-
    born,
and gave her a wedding
with death for a fate. She breathes
in terror on all
and flies on her way like a bee.

    [*Phaedra goes to the door of the palace and
    listens.*]

PHAEDRA

Be silent, women! O now, I am really ruined!

**CHORUS**

What is it, Phaedra, frightens you inside your house?

**PHAEDRA**

Be quiet. Let me hear the voice of those inside.

**CHORUS**

I will. Though this beginning seems to me not good.

**PHAEDRA**

Oh! Oh! alas! alas!
O wretched thing I am in these my sufferings!

**CHORUS**

What are the words you speak? What is the tale you tell?
Say what speech it is, my lady, that frightens you so,
tearing into your heart.

**PHAEDRA**

O I am lost! Just stand beside these gates, and there
listen to all the uproar falling on the house.

**CHORUS**

You are there by the door. You it is who must tell
of the words that come from within.
Tell me what can it be, what evil is here.

**PHAEDRA**

He shouts aloud, the son of the huntress Amazon,
Hippolytus, and to my nurse says dreadful things.

**CHORUS**

Yes, I can hear the voice; yet cannot clearly tell
whence came the cry to you,
came to you through the gates.

**PHAEDRA**

O listen, clearly now he calls her 'procuress
of evil and betrayer of her master's bed.'

**CHORUS**

O, I weep for your pain. Lady, you are betrayed.
How can I find you help?
Secret things are revealed, and you are lost . . .

**PHAEDRA**

Alas! Alas!

By your friends betrayed.

PHAEDRA
She has destroyed me, telling him of my distress,
kindly, not nobly, seeking to relieve my pain.

CHORUS
What now? What will you do, caught so much in a trap?

PHAEDRA
I do not know, except for one thing,—that quick death
remains the only cure for all my present pain.
[*Phaedra retires. Hippolytus, with the Nurse
following him, comes in.*]

HIPPOLYTUS
O mother Earth and you unfoldings of the sun,
I have heard the unspeakable sound of most foul words.

NURSE
Be silent, child, lest someone notice your cries.

HIPPOLYTUS
I have heard dreadful things. How can I hold my tongue?

NURSE
I beg you, by this right hand of yours, and this strong
arm.

HIPPOLYTUS
Take your hands off me! Do not dare to touch my clothes.

NURSE
I implore you by your knees. Do not be my ruin.

HIPPOLYTUS
How can I, if, as you pretend, your words were good?

NURSE
O child, this story is not fit for all to hear.

HIPPOLYTUS
More hearers the more honour, when the news is good.

NURSE
O child, you must respect the oath you swore to me.

It was my tongue that swore: my mind has made no oath.

**NURSE**
O child, what will you do? Will you destroy your friends?

**HIPPOLYTUS**
Your words revolt me. No bad person is my friend.

**NURSE**
Have pity! It is natural, my child, to make mistakes.

**HIPPOLYTUS**
O Zeus, why did you house them in the light of day,
women, man's evil, a false glittering counterfeit?
For if you wished to propagate the race of men,
this should not have been brought about by women's
    means.
Instead men should have offered in exchange their wealth
within your temples,—gold or silver or a weight
of bronze,—and bought their children for the price they
    paid,
each at its proper value. And then they could live
in free and easy homes and have no need of wives.
This makes it clear how great an evil a woman is:
the father who breeds and educates one pays a dowry too
that she may live elsewhere and he be free from pain.
And then the man who takes this curse inside his house
delights in adding fine adornments to her shape,
worthless itself, spends time in finding dresses for her,
the fool, and wastes away the substance of his house.
He's in a cleft stick; for, if he can marry well
and likes his new relations, then his wife will be
a bitter thing; and, if his wife is good, he'll find
worthless relations, bad and good luck counterpoised.
Easiest for him who has settled in his home a wife
whose mind's a total blank, a simple useless thing.
I hate a clever woman, and in my house never would
have one with more ideas than women ought to have.
For Cypris inculcates more often evil ways
among the clever ones, whereas the helpless kind
are barred from loose behaviour by their lack of wit.

No servant ever should have access to a wife:
their company should be some biting speechless beast,
so that they could not even speak to anyone,
nor get an answer back from those whom they address.
But as it is wives who are bad make their bad plots
at home, and then their servants carry them outside.
Like you, you miserable wretch, who came to me
to make arrangements for my father's sacred bed.
With running water I shall wash my ears and wipe
away your words. How could I ever be so base,
I, who, just hearing you, must think myself unclean?
Be sure what saves you, woman, is my sense of right.
If, carelessly, I had not bound myself by oaths,
for sure I should have told my father of all this.
And now, so long as Theseus is away from home,
I shall be absent too, and keep a silent tongue;
and then, returning with my father, I shall watch
how you will meet his eye, you and your mistress too.
Yes, I shall know, having tasted of your shamelessness.
I would destroy you all,—never shall have enough
of hating women, though they say that I'm always
saying the same thing. Women too are always bad.
Either let someone teach them to be self-controlled
or else allow me still to tread them under foot.

[*Hippolytus goes out. Phaedra comes forward.*]

PHAEDRA

O sad they are, unlucky,
the fates that women have!
Now that our hopes are betrayed, what art
what words can we find to loose the knot of his speech?
The verdict is given. O earth, and light!
Where can I go to escape my fate?
How, dear friends, can I hide my pain?
Which of the gods would succour me now? What man
can appear to stand beside me as fellow worker
in evil deeds? O no, my life's disaster
stays with me still and cannot be escaped.
I am the most unlucky one of women.

CHORUS

Alas! it is all over. They miscarried, those

arts of your servant, lady. Things are bad indeed.

PHAEDRA [*to the Nurse*]

You wicked woman, you destroyer of your friends,
what have you done to me? I pray my parent Zeus
may blot you out entirely with a blow of fire!
Did I not tell you, seeing in advance your mind,
to make no mention of what now has brought me shame?
But you had no restraint, and now no longer can I die
with a good name. I greatly need some new device.
Hippolytus, with anger sharpening his mind,
will speak against me, tell his father of your sins,
and tell the aged Pittheus of my sufferings,
and fill the whole land with the shameful story of it.
My curse on you, and on all those who are so keen
to help friends in dishonest ways against their will!

NURSE

You, lady, can reproach me for the wrong I did;
the hurt you feel is stronger than your power to judge.
Yet I too can reply to this, if you will hear.
I brought you up and seek your good. I tried to find
medicine for your disease, and found not what I wished.
Had I been lucky, I should have been thought most wise
since brains are measured by the way events fall out.

PHAEDRA

Is this your sense of right and proper speech to me,—
to wound me first, and then admit as much in words?

NURSE

Our speeches are too long. I have been indiscreet.
Yet from all this, my child, there is a safe way out.

PHAEDRA

Stop talking. You have given me before advice
that was dishonest, and your action too was bad.
So now begone out of my sight, think of yourself;
and I shall act with honour in my own affairs.
And now I ask you, noble daughters of Troezen,
to listen to my prayers and grant me this request,—
to hide in silence all that you have heard of here.

CHORUS

I swear by mighty Artemis, the child of Zeus,

101

not ever to bring any of your woes to light.

PHAEDRA

You have spoken fairly. Now, searching my mind, I find
one way and one alone to meet my present pass,
so as to leave my children honour in their lives
and help myself in what has happened to me now.
For I shall never put my Cretan home to shame
or, after these disgraceful doings, come within
the sight of Theseus, just to save one single life.

CHORUS

What evil without cure do you intend to do?

PHAEDRA

To die; but how to die is what I now shall plan.

CHORUS

O do not say such words!

PHAEDRA

You must give good advice.
In parting from my life upon this very day
I shall give joy to Cypris who is destroying me.
Bitter has been the love which brings me my defeat,
yet I, in death, shall prove at least an evil thing
to another, so that he may learn not to be proud
in my misfortune. He will have a share with me
in this complaint of mine, and so learn modest ways.

[*Phaedra goes into the palace.*]

CHORUS

O I would be in aerial hiding-places,
that a god might set me there in the flying flocks,
myself a bird on the wing!
I would be borne on high
to the waves of the sea on the Adriatic shore,
to Eridanus' waters, where
into the dark-blue stream,
pitying Phaethon, the luckless Heliades
melt in their bright and amber-shining tears.

Or might I make my way to the apple gardens
102

of the singing Hesperides, where the dark sea's lord
ends the journeys of ships!
There he dwells in the terrible
verge of heaven that Atlas holds with his arms,
and ambrosial fountains flow
from the resting places of Zeus,
from his palace halls where life-giving holy earth
still for the gods increases their happiness.

White-winged vessel from Crete
that, through the salt of the wave and the beat of the sea
bore my mistress away from her happy home
with a prize of unfortunate love!
Surely ill-starred both ways, or at least from Crete,
to famous Athens it winged its way,
and there on Munychian shores
they tied the ends of their twisted ropes
and set their feet on the land.

For that Aphrodite broke
her heart with the terrible sickness of passion impure.
Now, since she is overladen with hard events,
she will tie to her bridal roof
the hanging noose of a rope, and fit it tight
to the white of her neck, being filled with shame
at the face of the hateful goddess.
First she will choose good fame and to rid
her heart of the pains of love.
    [A Servant is heard crying out inside the palace.]

SERVANT

Oh! Oh!
Come here and help, all you that are about the house!
Our mistress and the wife of Theseus is hanged.

CHÓRUS

Alas! Alas! It is all over, now no more
the royal lady lives, hanged in the swinging noose.

SERVANT

Be quick! Let someone bring a knife with double edge
with which we can unloose the knot about her neck.

103

## CHORUS

What should we do, my friends? Do you think we
    should go
inside and loose our lady from the choking rope?

## SEMI-CHORUS

Why should we? Are there not young men as servants
    there?
By being over-zealous we may risk our lives.

## SERVANT

Set the limbs straight, and so lay out this wretched body.
Sad for my master is this housekeeping of hers.

## CHORUS

Now she is dead, I hear it, this unhappy woman.
Already they lay out her body as a corpse.

*[Enter Theseus with his attendants. Since he has
been on some religious journey, he is wearing a
garland on his head.]*

## THESEUS

Do you know, women, what this uproar means indoors?
A noise of wailing from my servants reached my ears.
Strange that they do not think it right to unbar the gates
and kindly greet me back from my religious way.
Surely no ill has happened to aged Pittheus?
He is already far advanced in life, yet still,
were he to leave us, it would be a grief to me.

## CHORUS

Theseus, this is a thing that does not touch the old.
It is the death of youth that will bring pain to you.

## THESEUS

Alas! Not that my children's life is stolen away?

## CHORUS

They live. Their mother,—sad, most sad for you—is dead.

## THESEUS

What do you say? My wife dead? How then did she die?

## CHORUS

She fastened up a running noose to hang herself.

**THESEUS**

Had grief frozen her blood, or did some evil come to her?

**CHORUS**

So much I know, no more. I too have only just,
Theseus, approached your house in mourning for your
    loss.

**THESEUS**

Ah, why then have I set this crown of woven leaves
upon my head, unlucky in my holy voyage?
Come, men, undo the bolts that bar the double doors!
Loosen the chains, that I may see this bitter sight
of my dead wife who, by her death, has destroyed me.
    [*The doors are opened and the body of Phaedra
    is discovered.*]

**CHORUS**

Oh, alas, poor lady, your pitiful fate!
You have suffered and done
a deed that can utterly ruin this house.
O reckless your doing, this violent death
in the sinful event, overthrown,
O pitiful, by your own hand!
Which god, my poor lady, has taken the light from your
    life?

**THESEUS**

O I weep for my pain! O my city, this is
the worst of the things I have suffered. O fate,
how heavy have you fallen on me and my house,
a spreading stain unknown from some avenging power,
or rather a murderer's blow taking the life from my life.
And an ocean of evil, poor wretch, is in front of my eyes
so great that I can never more swim clear of it
nor cross beyond the wave of this catastrophe.
Alas! my wife, what word can I find,
how can I name your burden of fate?
For like a bird you slipped out of the hand away
from me and leaped a sheer leap to the house of death.
O how pitiful is this suffering! O, alas!
Out of the past somewhere I am reaping the fate

sent by a god for the sins
of someone who lived of old.

My lord, these evils have not come to you alone.
You have lost a worthy wife, and so have many more.

THESEUS

Below the earth, in the cloud that's below the earth
I wish to dwell in the dark, I wish to die,
now separated from your dear companionship;
for, perishing, you have destroyed more than yourself.
O, what news can I hear? Whence, poor wife, did it come,
the fate of death to your heart?
Can someone tell me what was done? Or does my royal
    house
uselessly shelter numbers of my serving men?
O, my heart aches for you!
O I pity the grief I have seen in my home.
It is not to be borne and not to be told. I am lost.
My home is empty and my children motherless.
You have left me, left me behind,
dearest of women and best that the ray of the sun
sees, or the star-faced moon in the night.

CHORUS

Alas, unhappy, the pain that fills the house!
Streaming with tears my eyes
melt for your fate. And for long
I tremble at the woe that will come next.

THESEUS

Ha!
What can this mean, this letter that is hanging down
from her dear hand? Has she some news she wants to tell?
Surely she has written down, poor thing, her will about
the children and my love, and made me some request.
Poor creature, be at rest! No woman in the world
will enter Theseus' bed or come within his house.
And now the prints of that gold signet ring she had,
she who no longer lives,—these seem to touch my heart.
Come, let me break the fastenings about the seals
and see what thing it is this letter wants to say.

Alas! Alas! Here now a god brings on
evil news in its turn. To me no fate
of life deserves to be lived after this that is done.
For I speak of our master's home, alas, alas,
as being destroyed, as being a thing of the past.
O god, if such there be, do not betray this house
but listen to my prayer; for, like a prophetess,
from omens I can see the evil on its way.

**THESEUS**

O what a fearful wrong upon the top of wrong!
Unspeakable, insufferable, O alas!

**CHORUS**

What is it? Speak if I may share the news at all.

**THESEUS**

This letter cries and cries what cannot be forgot.
Where can I leave my weight of woe? O, I am lost
    indeed,
utterly lost! What a speaking strain
in her writing I saw! Ah me!

**CHORUS**

Alas, the word you speak leads on the way to pain.

**THESEUS**

I can keep it no longer behind the gates of my lips,
this evil so deadly, so hard to be mended.
Oh, my city!
Hippolytus has dared to violate my bed
by force and shown contempt for Zeus's holy eye.
O now Poseidon, father, you who promised me
the power to curse three times, with one of these do you
destroy my son, and let him not survive this day.
Do this, if you indeed gave me the power to curse.

**CHORUS**

My lord, recall that curse, I beg you, back again.
Soon you will see that you were wrong. O listen to me!

**THESEUS**

It is impossible. And also I shall drive
him from this land. By one or other fate he will

be crushed. Either Poseidon, honouring my curse,
will end his life and send him to the gates of Hell,
or else, in exile from this land and wandering
abroad, he will live through a hard and bitter life.

[*Enter Hippolytus with his attendants.*]

### CHORUS

Look, here Hippolytus, your son, has come himself
at the right time. Relax your cruel anger, lord
Theseus, and make the best decision for your house.

### HIPPOLYTUS

I heard your cry, my father, and have come to you
with all speed. Yet I do not know what thing it is
for which you grieve. This I would like to learn from you.
O, what is this? My father, now I see your wife
lying dead there. This is a thing to wonder at.
She whom only just now I parted from, she who
not long ago was looking on the light of day!
What happened to her? In what way was she destroyed?
Father, it is from you I wish to learn of this.
You do not speak? Yet silence does no good in pain;
for, when the heart desires to hear of everything,
it must in trouble also be inquisitive.
Then, father, surely it cannot be right to hide
your misery from friends and even more than friends.

### THESEUS

O how men uselessly and often go astray!
Why give instruction in the many countless arts,
use all devices, make inventions of all kinds,
while one thing is not known and never studied yet—
to teach intelligence to those who have no sense?

### HIPPOLYTUS

Some clever expert you must mean, who has the power
to force to wisdom those who are deprived of it.
But, father, this is not the time for sophistry.
I fear your sufferings must have deranged your speech.

### THESEUS

Alas! there should have been for men some certain sign
to mark their friends, some way of reading in their minds
which one is true and which one not a friend at all;

everyone should have had two different tones of voice,
one for his plain just dealings, one for all the rest.
Then words from false minds could have been compared
    and judged
by what was true, and I should not have been deceived.

HIPPOLYTUS

No, surely none of my friends has spoken ill of me
into your ear? And, innocent, am I diseased?
Sir, I am all amazed, and what amazes me
is your strange words that seem to leave the path of sense.

THESEUS

O mind of man! To what lengths will it not proceed?
Where will a bound be set to reckless arrogance?
For if in every generation this swells up,
if the younger comes to an excess of shame beyond
the former generation, then the gods will have
to add another world to this one, which will hold
the evil men who are by nature all depraved.
Look at this young man here, who, though he is my son,
has brought pollution to my bed, and without doubt
is proved the greatest villain by this woman's death.
And now, since any way your presence stains the air,
turn your head here, and let your father see your face.
So you are he who, as a man marked out, consorts
with gods? You are the chaste one, all untouched by sin?
I certainly will not believe your boasting words
or be a fool to credit gods with ignorance.
Now boast away, try to impose on people with
your meatless meals, take Orpheus for your lord and join
the revel, worshipping the smoke of countless books.
You are found out. And people of your sort I bid
all men avoid. You are of those who seek their prey
by pompous language while you scheme your shameful
    deeds.
She's dead. And do you think that this will make you safe?
No, you mean creature. This is where you are most
    caught.
For where will you find oaths, where words to be more
    strong

for your acquittal than this argument of her?
You will pretend she hated you, and say bastards
and true-born children are by nature enemies.
That would suggest she bargained badly with her life,
through hating you to throw away what she loved best.
Or will you say that folly does not go with men
but is a part of woman's nature? I know well
young men no more reliable than women are
when Cypris brings confusion to their youthful hearts,
although they have advantages by being men.
But why should I thus meet you in a strife of words,
When this dead body here is surest evidence?
Go! Leave this land, an exile, quick as you can do,
and neither enter god-built Athens nor the bounds
of any country over which my spear holds sway.
I have suffered from you, and if I am worsted by you,
then Sinis of the Isthmus can deny the fact
I ever killed him, say it was an empty boast,
and Sciron's rocks that fall into the sea can say
I am not heavy on the doers of bad deeds.

### CHORUS

How can I say that anyone at all of men
is happy? What was first is overturned again.

### HIPPOLYTUS

Father, the rage and tension in your heart make me
afraid. As for the charge, there are good arguments,
yet, when examined, then it is not fair at all.
I have no skill at making speeches to a crowd
and am wiser with a few who are my own equals.
This too is natural. Those who among the wise
are fools show more intelligence in speaking to
a crowd. Yet, all the same, since I am in this pass,
I am bound to loose my tongue. And I shall start my
    speech
from where you first attacked me surreptitiously,
thinking to injure me and give me no reply.
You see this light and earth. In them there is not one,
deny it as you may, who is more pure than I.
For, first, I know how to give reverence to the gods
and to have friends who will not try to injure me,

110

whose sense of shame prevents them asking what is bad
or aiding their associates in wicked deeds.
I, father, do not mock at those with whom I live,
but, near or far, am still a friend in the same way.
One thing has never touched me,—what you think my
 guilt.
This body to this moment is unstained by love.
I do not know the action, except what I hear
in talk or see in pictures, and I have no wish
to know about such things. I have a virgin soul.
Perhaps my purity does not convince your mind.
Then you must show in what way I became corrupt.
Was it this woman's body was more beautiful
than that of all the rest? Or did I hope to make
your house my own by taking on an heiress' bed?
Could I be such a fool, so quite outside my mind?
Or do wise-minded men enjoy the sweets of power?
They do not. For, when power is absolute, it will
always corrupt the minds of men who feel its charm.
For me, I'd choose to win in the Hellenic games
first prize, and in my city be the second man,
and so live happy always with my noble friends.
This means an active life with no danger attached,
and gives more pleasure than life of supreme power.

 One thing in my defence I have not said. The rest
you know. But, if I had a witness like myself,
and if this woman saw the light when I was tried,
then, looking at the evidence, you would have seen
which was the guilty. Now, I swear to you by Zeus,
guardian of oaths, by earth's floor, that I never touched
your wife, nor could have wished to, nor conceived the
 thought.
And may I die inglorious, without a name,
without a house or city, exiled and wandering,
and, after death, let neither sea nor land receive
my body, if in truth I am a wicked man.
And, if it was from terror that she threw away
her life, I do not know. More than this I must not say.
She has controlled herself, though lacking in the power;
I have the power, but have made bitter use of it.

**CHORUS**

You have said enough to turn away the charge from you,
swearing an oath, no small conviction, to the gods.

**THESEUS**

Is he some wizard or enchanter who believes
that by his even temper he can get his way
over my spirit, after having wronged his sire?

**HIPPOLYTUS**

This too in you, my father, fills me with surprise.
If I had been your father and you been my son,
I should have killed you, not punished you with exile,
if you had dared to lay your hands upon my wife.

**THESEUS**

That is just like you. No, you shall not die like this,
according to the law you frame to suit yourself.
For a quick death is easiest for wicked men.
But, wandering in exile from your father's land,
abroad you will live through a hard and bitter life.
For this is the correct reward for wicked men.

**HIPPOLYTUS**

Alas! What will you do? Will you not wait for time
to inform against me? Will you drive me from the land?

**THESEUS**

Yes, and beyond the sea and bounds that Atlas made,
if I might do it, so I hate the sight of you.

**HIPPOLYTUS**

Will you not test the truth by oaths or guarantees
or words of seers, but banish me without a trial?

**THESEUS**

This letter here, with no prophetic stamp on it,
is evidence enough against you. As for birds
that flit above my head, I take no stock of that.

**HIPPOLYTUS**

O gods, why then can I not loose my lips,
I who by you am ruined, you whom I revere?
I cannot. Even then I'd fail to move the minds
I should move, and would vainly break the oath I swore.

**THESEUS**

Oh, these grand airs of yours will drive me to my grave!
Will you not go, and leave at once your father's house?

**HIPPOLYTUS**

O where then can I turn, poor wretch? Which of my
    friends
will take me to his house, exiled on such a charge?

**THESEUS**

One who enjoys receiving guests who will defile
other men's wives and take their share in deeds of shame.

**HIPPOLYTUS**

Ah! This goes to my heart and brings me near to tears,
that I should look so bad and you should think me so.

**THESEUS**

This time to groan and feel the future was the time
you dared commit an outrage on your father's wife.

**HIPPOLYTUS**

O palace, how I wish that you would cry aloud
for me, and witness whether I am really bad!

**THESEUS**

You wisely look for witnesses that have no voice.

    [*He points to the dead body.*]

This fact that does not speak proclaims your wickedness.

**HIPPOLYTUS**

Alas!
I wish that I could stand in front of my own self
and see my face. I would have wept for what I feel.

**THESEUS**

Yes, you are much more trained in worshipping yourself
than in honouring your father with an honest mind.

**HIPPOLYTUS**

O my poor mother, bitter was your birth of me!
Let bastards never be among the friends I have!

**THESEUS**

Drag him out, slaves! Do you not hear? For long
I have been ordering this man to leave my land.

#### HIPPOLYTUS

The first of them who touches me will suffer for it.
Thrust me away yourself, if this is what you will.

#### THESEUS

That is what I shall do, if you will not obey.
No trace of pity for your exile touches me.

[*Exit Theseus.*]

#### HIPPOLYTUS

Then it is fixed, it seems. O, what a wretch I am!
I know the truth, but do not know how I can speak.
O child of Leto, dearest to me of the gods,
who rested with me, hunted with me, must I leave
great Athens as an exile? O farewell, you land
and city of Erechtheus! O, Troezenian plains,
what happiness you gave me as I grew up here!
Farewell! I see you for the last time as I speak.
Now come, my friends and young companions of this
  land,
speak to me now and see me on my way abroad.
Never will you behold a man more pure than I,
even although my father does not think it so.

[*Exit Hippolytus with his friends and attendants.*]

#### CHORUS

Greatly indeed it will ease me of grief, when it comes to
  my mind,
the thought of the gods.
Yet, though guessing in hope at their wisdom,
I am downcast again when I look at the fortunes and
  actions of mortals,
for they alter, now here and now there;
man's life has no fixed station
but is mutable always.

I wish when I make my prayers this fate from the gods
  might be mine—
to have wealth for my lot
and a heart unacquainted with grief.

114

And the thoughts in my mind should not be too subtle,
    nor counterfeit either;
but, easily willing to alter
my ways as the morrow comes,
I should always be happy.

No more can I look with a mind undisturbed upon things
    unexpected,
now the brightest of stars
of Hellas, of Athens,—we saw it—
is sent by the rage of his father
to foreign countries abroad.
O sands of the shores of my city,
O glades in the mountains where he
slew wild beasts with his swift-footed hounds,
and holy Dictynna was with him!

No more will you stand in the chariot drawn by Venetian
    fillies
on the Limnean track,
holding in with your foot the wild horses.
And the sleepless strain of the lyre
will cease in your father's house.
Unwreathed in the green of the forest
are the coverts of Leto's child.
In your exile the contest is ended
of maidens who vied for your love.

O for your misfortune I shall pass
in tears my ill-fated fate.
Useless, poor mother, was your birth of him.
My anger falls on the gods.
Alas, you band of the Graces,
why have you sent him away
from this house, from his native land,
he, quite without guilt in this evil?

    [A *Messenger, one of Hippolytus' attendants*
    *approaches.*]

**CHORUS**

But now I see one of Hippolytus' men.
He comes up to the house in haste with a wild look.

**MESSENGER**

Women, which is the way for me to go to find
Theseus, this country's king? If you know where he is,
then tell me of it. Is he now inside the house?

**CHORUS**

I see him there coming himself outside the house.

**MESSENGER**

Theseus, I bring you tidings that will make you think,
you and your citizens that live in Athens' town
and in the boundaries of this Troezenian land.

**THESEUS**

What is it? Can it be that some fresh blow of fate
has come upon these twin and neighbouring towns of
    mine?

**MESSENGER**

Let me speak plain. Hippolytus no more exists.
He sees the light, but life is hanging by a thread.

**THESEUS**

Who killed him? Was it one who hated him because
his wife, like mine, was violated and defiled?

**MESSENGER**

It was the chariot he drove that caused his death;
that, and the curses from your mouth which you called
    down
from the sea's governor, your father, on your son.

**THESEUS**

Gods! O Poseidon, so in very truth you were
my father, since you heard the prayer I made to you!
How did he die? Tell me. What was the way in which
the trap of Justice closed on him who shamed me so?

**MESSENGER**

We were beside the promontory where the waves
beat on the shore, and combing down the horses' manes,
weeping, because a messenger had come to say

116

that now no longer must Hippolytus set foot
within this land, condemned by you to sad exile.
And then he came himself with the same strain of tears
to us upon the shore, and at his heels there came
with him a countless band of friends of his own age.
For long he did not cease lamenting. Then he said:
'Why do I rave? My father's words must be obeyed.
Prepare my yoke of horses for the chariot,
attendants. In this city I have no more right.'
And then each one of us pressed onward with the work,
and, quicker than it takes to tell, we had the mares
standing all ready harnessed in our master's sight.
Then from the chariot rail he snatches up the reins,
plants his feet firmly in the sockets on the floor,
and, stretching out his hands, he first addressed the gods:
'O Zeus, if I am sinful, let me cease to live,
and let my father know that he is wronging me
either when I am dead or while I see the light.'
And straight away he took into his hands the goad
and laid it on the horses, while we men ran on
close to the chariot's reins in escort to our lord,
on the straight road to Argos and Epidaurus.
Now, when we reached the open country just beyond
the frontier of this land, there is a stretch of shore
that lies already facing the Saronic gulf.
Here from the ground a roar like Zeus' thunderclap
came sounding heavy round us, terrible to hear.
The horses raised their heads and pricked their ears
        right up
into the air, and on us fell a lively fear,
wondering what the sound could be. And when we looked
along the foaming shores, we saw a monstrous wave
towering up to the sky, so big it took away
the view of Sciron's promontory from my eyes.
It hid the Isthmus and Asclepius' rock.
Next, swelling up and surging onward, with, all round,
a mass of foam, and with the roaring of the sea,
it neared the shore where stood the four-horse chariot.
And, in the very surge and breaking of the flood,
the wave threw up a bull, a fierce and monstrous thing,
and with his bellowing the land was wholly filled,

117

and fearful re-echoed. As for us who saw
the sight, it seemed too much for eyes to look upon.
Immediately a dreadful panic seized the steeds.
My master, with his long experience of how
horses behave, gripped tightly in his hands the reins
and pulled upon them, like a boatman pulls his oar,
knotting the straps behind him and leaning back on them.
But the horses, taking in their teeth the fiery bits,
carried him on by force and took no care at all
either of master hand or of the knotted reins
or of the welded chariot; and, if he steered their course,
as with a tiller, to the smoother bits of ground,
then in their faces there appeared, to turn them back,
the bull, and drove the four-horse team all mad with fear.
And, if they rushed with maddened minds upon the rocks,
he silently drew near the chariot, and ran
alongside, till, forcing the wheel against a stone,
he overthrew the car and hurled the driver out.
Then all was huddled in a mass. The naves of wheels
and axle pins together flew into the air.
Hippolytus himself, entangled in the reins,
tied in inextricable bonds, was dragged along,
his dear head dashed upon the rocks, his flesh all torn,
and crying out words terrible for us to hear.
'O stop, you horses that were fed within my stalls!
Do not wipe out my life! Alas, my father's curse!
Will no one come to me and save a noble man?'
And many of us longed to do so, but we were
left far behind. Yet in the end he was set free
somehow or other from the bonds of these fine reins,
and fell down with a little life left in him still.
The horses and that awful monster of a bull
had disappeared somewhere along the rocky ground.
My lord, I am a slave within your house, and yet
this is a thing that I shall never be induced
to think,—that your son really was a wicked man:
no, not if all the race of women hung themselves,
or if all Ida's pines were filled with written words,
I'd not believe it, since I know that he is good.

**CHORUS**

Now the disaster of fresh evil is fulfilled.

From fate and from necessity there's no escape.

In hatred for the man who met this fate I was
pleased with your news. But now I feel a reverent awe
both towards the gods and him, since he was born of me;
and by these evils I am neither pleased nor grieved.

MESSENGER
What are we now to do to please you? Shall we bring
this suffering creature here, or what are we to do?
Think carefully. And my advice to you would be
not to be cruel to your own son in his pain.

THESEUS
Bring him to me, that I may see before my eyes
him who denied that he had made my bed his own,
that I by words and acts of gods may prove him wrong.

CHORUS
The unbending minds of gods and men,
Cypris, are prisoners to you,
and with you goes on wheeling swiftest wing
the gleaming feathered god.
He flies above the earth, above
the salt resounding sea.
Love brings enchantment when in shine of gold
and winged he comes upon the maddened heart.
He charms the tribes of mountain beasts,
beasts of the sea and all that earth supplies,
all creatures brightened by the seeing sun;
men too, and, Cypris, you alone
rule over all with sovereign power.

[*The goddess Artemis appears.*]

ARTEMIS
You I address and bid you to listen,
great son of Aigeus!
The daughter of Leto, I, Artemis, speak to you.
Why are you foolishly pleased with this, Theseus,
you who have wickedly murdered your son,
led to believe by your wife's false words
uncertain things? You have gained certain ruin.

119

How you would wish in the depths of the earth
to hide your body in shame, or, changing
your life to the air, be a bird and keep far
away from this pain!
Since among good men there is certainly
no lot in life for you.
Hear, Theseus, now the state of ill in which you are.
Be sure I do not gain from it and I shall cause you pain.
But for this reason I have come, to make you see
how your son's heart was pure, that he may die with fame,
and make you see the savage passion of your wife
or, in a way, the nobleness; for she was pricked
by sting of that most hateful of the gods to us
who love a virgin life, and she desired your son.
She tried by resolution to beat Cypris down,
and then was lost, unwilling, by her nurse's craft,
who under oath informed your son of her disease.
And he, just as was right, neither was influenced
by what she said, nor, when by you he was maligned,
would break his pledged word, since his nature fears
    the gods.
But she, your wife, in fear lest she might be found out,
Wrote a false story down and by this trick of hers
destroyed your son, yet all the same persuaded you.

THESEUS

Alas!

ARTEMIS

Does the tale, Theseus, bite your heart? Yet quietly wait
and hear what follows, that you may lament still more.
You know you have three certain curses from your sire,
and one of them, you wicked man, you have misused
against your son. It might have been against a foe.
Your father, the sea's king, with honourable mind,
gave what he had to give since he had promised it.
But both to him and me your wickedness is clear.
You did not wait for guarantees or words of seers,
made no examination, nor by course of time
allowed enquiry, but, more quickly than you ought,
you laid the curse upon your son and took his life.

O lady, I am lost.

Your deed is dreadful. Yet
still there may be forgiveness here even for you.
It was the will of Cypris that these things should be,
to sate her rage. There is this rule among the gods,—
that none of us will check another god's desire
when it is shown. Instead we always stand aside.
Be sure that if I did not fear the power of Zeus
I never would have sunk to such a depth of shame
as to allow the death of him who is to me
dearest of men. As for your sin, first the fact
of ignorance frees you from guilt of evil thought.
And then your wife, who now is dead, poured out her
    words
of evidence so much that they persuaded you.
And on you chiefly now has broken all this ill,
but I too feel the pain. The gods do not rejoice
when good men die. As for the wicked, we destroy
them, and their houses and the children that they have.

[*Hippolytus is carried in by his attendants.*]

See! Here the wretched sufferer comes.
His youthful flesh and golden hair
have lost their beauty. O what pain,
what double grief has fallen on these halls
and swooped on them from heaven!

Alas! Alas!
I in my misery all disfigured
by unjust curse of an unjust father,
I am destroyed. Alas! Alas!
Through my head goes a darting anguish,
spasms leap within my brain.
Stop! Let me rest my weary body.
Hateful my chariot, hateful my horses
fed from my hand!
You have slain and destroyed me.

O, my servants, gently, I beg you
touch my bruised flesh with your hands!
Who is it standing there at my right side?
Lift me up carefully, raise me together,
me the unfortunate, me the cursed one
by fault of my father. O Zeus, do you see it?
I who was holy, I who was reverent,
I who surpassed all men in my purity,
am going to certain death under ground,
losing my life. O useless the efforts
I made out of kindness
in service to men!
Oh! Oh!
It is the pain, the pain coming over me.
Leave me to suffer!
O let Death, the Healer, come for me!
O you are killing me, doubling my pain.
How I long for a two-edged spear blade
to cut through my body
and bring my life to its rest!
O sad the curse my father laid upon me.
It is the sin of bloody ancestors,
of forefathers in ancient times, that comes
down from the past on me and will not stay.
Yet why on me all guiltless of these sins?
Alas, what should I say?
How can I free my life from this
insufferable pain?
O let the black of death and night of fate
lull me, unhappy, to my sleep!

ARTEMIS

Poor youth, how you are yoked together with your pain!
It was the goodness of your heart destroyed your life.

HIPPOLYTUS

Ha!
O heavenly breath of fragrance! Even in my pains
I feel your presence, and my body grows more light.
Is Artemis, the goddess, present in this place?

122

**ARTEMIS**

Poor youth, she is, and loves you more than all the gods.

**HIPPOLYTUS**

You see me, lady, and my state, my wretched state?

**ARTEMIS**

I see you, but my eyes are not allowed to weep.

**HIPPOLYTUS**

No more the huntsman for you and the serving man . . .

**ARTEMIS**

No more. Yet in your dying you are dear to me.

**HIPPOLYTUS**

No more to guard your statues or to drive your steeds.

**ARTEMIS**

No. It was cruel Cypris wished these things to be.

**HIPPOLYTUS**

Alas! I recognise the god who took my life.

**ARTEMIS**

Jealous of honour, angry at your living pure.

**HIPPOLYTUS**

Alone, I see, she has destroyed all three of us.

**ARTEMIS**

Yes. You, your father, and his wife, the third of you.

**HIPPOLYTUS**

Then I must weep too for my father's sufferings.

**ARTEMIS**

It was the counsel of a god deceived his mind.

**HIPPOLYTUS**

Unhappy father in this suffering of yours!

**THESEUS**

My son. I am destroyed and have no joy in life.

**HIPPOLYTUS**

More than myself, I grieve for you and your mistake.

**THESEUS**

I wish that I, my child, could die instead of you.

**HIPPOLYTUS**

Bitter the gifts your sire, Poseidon, gave to you.

**THESEUS**

I wish that it had never mounted to my lips.

**HIPPOLYTUS**

Why so? You would have killed me, angry as you were.

**THESEUS**

Yes, for the gods had cheated me of my good sense.

**HIPPOLYTUS**

Alas!
I wish the race of men had power to curse the gods.

**ARTEMIS**

Be satisfied. For no, not in the dark of earth
shall I allow, at Cypris' pleasure, rage to light
upon your body unavenged; and this because
of your godfearingness and of your noble mind.
For I shall take from her with my own hand the one
of mortals whom above all others she loves best,
and so with my unerring bow become avenged.
And now on you, unhappy one, for all your pains
I shall bestow the greatest honours in this land
of Troezen. For unmarried girls, before they wed,
shall cut their hair to do you honour. You will have
for ages long the harvest of their mourning tears.
And always among maidens there will be desire
to make their songs of you. It will not pass away
or nameless sink to silence, Phaedra's love for you.
And you, O child of aged Aigeus, I bid take
your son up in your arms and give him your embrace.
It was against your will you slew him, and it is
natural for men to err when gods point out the way.
And you, Hippolytus, I counsel not to hate
your father, for you know the fate by which you died.
Farewell! For I am not allowed to see the dead,
or stain my eye with the last gasps of dying men,
and you I see already near that evil thing.

**HIPPOLYTUS**

O farewell, blessed maiden, go upon your way.

Easily now you leave our long companionship.
I end my quarrel with my father, as you bid,
and as in old times also I obeyed your words.

[*Artemis goes out.*]

Ah! Ah! Already darkness settles on my eyes.
Take hold of me, my father. Keep my body straight.

THESEUS

My son, what are you doing to me in my pain?

HIPPOLYTUS

Now I am dying. Now I see the gates of Hell.

THESEUS

O will you leave me here with heart unpurified?

HIPPOLYTUS

I will not, since I free you from the stain of blood.

THESEUS

What? You will set me free from guilt of shedding blood?

HIPPOLYTUS

I call the archer Artemis to witness it.

THESEUS

Dear son, how noble to your father's eyes you are.

HIPPOLYTUS

Pray that your true-born children may be like to me.

THESEUS

I weep for your good heart, your true and upright mind.

HIPPOLYTUS

Farewell to you too, father! O, a long farewell!

THESEUS

O my son, do not leave me! Summon up your strength.

HIPPOLYTUS

My strength is done and finished, father, and I die.
Now quickly with my garments hide away my face.

[*Hippolytus dies.*]

THESEUS

O famous bounds of Athens and of Pallas' land,
How great a man is this that you will lose! Alas!

How often, Cypris, shall I think of your ill deeds!

This is a grief that is common to all of us.
and came unexpected.
Many the tears that now will be falling,
since for great men mourning voices
still last longer.

# The HELEN
## of
# EURIPIDES

# THE CHARACTERS

HELEN, *wife of Menelaus*

TEUCER, *a Greek hero from the Trojan War*

MENELAUS, *King of Sparta and Greek leader in the Trojan War*

AN OLD WOMAN, *doorkeeper in the palace of Theoclymenus*

FIRST MESSENGER, *one of Menelaus' shipwrecked crew*

THEONOE, *a priestess and prophetess, sister of Theoclymenus*

THEOCLYMENUS, *King of Egypt*

SECOND MESSENGER, *one of Theoclymenus' sailors*

THE DIOSCURI, *the divine brothers of Helen (Castor and Pollux)*

CHORUS OF GREEK WOMEN, *prisoners in Egypt*

SAILORS, ATTENDANTS, HUNTSMEN, PRIESTS *and* PRIESTESSES

# Introduction

THE BACKGROUND TO the plot of this play is, as is usual with Euripides, carefully and distinctly explained in the first speech, or prologue. The audience would be immediately aware that Euripides was following not the Homeric account of Helen, but the story which is associated with the lyric poet Stesichorus, who lived about 600 B.C. This poet is supposed first to have written of Helen in the conventional manner as of a faithless wife who had, by involving her countrymen in the Trojan war, done much harm. On the basis of Homer's story such an account seems reasonable enough, but, unfortunately for Stesichorus, Helen was not only a woman but a goddess. He was therefore inflicted with blindness as a punishment for his insulting language. The quick-witted poet however soon recovered his sight by writing a famous recantation or 'Palinode' in which he stated that his previous poem could have had no basis in fact since Helen never really went to Troy at all. It was only her phantom that went there. How he developed this theme we do not know. As the real Helen could scarcely have remained unobserved in Sparta while her phantom was being fought for in Troy, it is probable that his version of the story was much the same as that of Euripides, who makes Helen the innocent victim of the rivalry between Hera and Aphrodite. She is transported by the gods to Egypt and left there while her husband and the Greeks go on fighting for her phantom year after year at Troy. So far as this part of the story goes it appears that Hera gets her revenge on Aphrodite by so arranging matters that Paris does not in fact receive the bribe he had been offered at the famous beauty contest on Mount Ida. Aphrodite on the other hand might claim to have fulfilled her promise since what Paris did receive was indistinguishable from what he did not. [This particular aspect of the real and the phantom Helens is about the only one which Euripides does not exploit.] A more serious motive for the action of the Gods is the whole question of the Trojan war, which is fated or designed either from divine enmity to the Trojans or as a means to rid the earth of surplus population.

With this basis to his story Euripides with his human actors has composed a play which is more like a romantic comedy than what we usually think of as 'tragedy.' There is all the fun that can possibly be extracted from mistaken identity and from scenes of recognition. There is a chase and an escape and a happy ending. Though both Helen and Menelaus are constantly reverting to their past sufferings, in the actual play no one suffers at all. Even Theoclymenus, the duped and disappointed barbarian suitor, seems quite easily reconciled with his lot. Indeed, so far as the main characters are concerned, it seems to be simply an exciting play on the theme of virtue rewarded and real identity revealed.

Yet the play is not precisely a comedy. In at least two respects Euripides is taking his subject seriously. In the first place there is the character of Helen herself. Euripides had been reproached often enough for his 'bad' women—his Phaedras and Medeas. Here he seems deliberately to be trying to create a 'good' woman, faithful through all kinds of dangers and temptations, not only beautiful but intelligent. True that at the very end of the play Theoclymenus, speaking of 'Helen's noble mind' states that this is 'a thing that in most women is not found at all.' Yet Euripides has produced one example where the quality of noble mindedness, however rare, does exist. Helen is a genuine heroine, not a subject for psychological study.

Perhaps Euripides is more serious still in his treatment of the whole idea of war, and this play, in spite of its lightness, is among the most 'pacifist' of his works. The play was probably produced in 412 B.C. at the time of the Athenian disasters in Sicily, disasters from which the Athenian imperial democracy never recovered. The themes of going to war for the sake of a phantom, of the advantages of negotiation rather than force in international affairs—these recur constantly in the play and must have been applied by the audience to the contemporary situation.

Thus there is a keen edge to much that might appear as merely humorous, and it is easier for us in our days to appreciate this than it was for nineteenth-century critics.

130

# THE HELEN OF EURIPIDES

*[The scene is in Egypt, before the
King's palace. Near the palace gates
there is a tomb or monument to the
old King of Egypt, Proteus. Helen is
standing by this tomb.]*

HELEN

THESE ARE the shining virgin streams of the river Nile
who, with the white snow melting, takes the place of rain
from heaven and waters all of Egypt's level fields.
Proteus was, while he lived, the ruler of this land.
King of all Egypt, though he lived in Pharos' isle.
He for his wife took one of the nymphs of the sea,
Psamathe, who had once been the wife of Aiacus.
She bore two children to this house, and one, the male,
was called 'Theoclymenus',—'God-honoured'—since his
    father's life
was spent in piety; the noble girl was called
Eido, or 'mother's pride', while she was still a child;
but when she reached the age when she might be a wife,
they called her 'Theonoe',—'God-inspired'—She knew
divinely what is present and what still to come,
having this as a gift from her grandfather, Nereus.
And as for me, my native land is not unknown,
Sparta its name, and Tyndarus my father,—though
there is a story that Zeus took upon himself
a swan's shape and then flew to my mother Leda
with an eagle in pursuit, and so made love to her
by a trick. That is the story, whether true or false.
My name is Helen, and the troubles I have had
are these: three goddesses for beauty's sake once came
to Paris in a hollow glade on Ida's hill,
Hera and Cypris and the virgin sprung from Zeus,
desiring from him final judgment on their charms.
And Cypris used my beauty as a bribe [if what
brings such bad luck is beauty] offering him me
as wife. And so she won, and Paris left his herds
and came to Sparta, certain to enjoy my love.
But Hera, angry, that she had not won first place,

131

loosed on the wind the love that Paris had from me;
it was not me she gave him, but she made like me
a breathing image, forming it from air, and this
she gave King Priam's son. He thought indeed he had
me for his own. He had not. What he thought was wrong.
And then on these misfortunes by the will of Zeus
more came. He brought down war upon the land of Greece
and on the unfortunate Trojans, so to lighten mother earth
of the excessive numbers of her men, and make
Achilles famous as the strongest Greek of all.
And there was I,—not I indeed, but just my name—
the ward of Trojan strength and prize for Grecian spears.
As for myself, Hermes took me in folds of air,
covering me with a cloud, for Zeus took care for me.
He brought me here and set me down in Proteus' house,
[of all men judging him to be most self-controlled]
that I might keep myself for Menelaus chaste.
So here I am. But meanwhile my poor husband raised
army and fleet together and set out to track
me and my captors to the towers of Ilium.
Many because of me beside Scamander's streams
Have lost their lives, and I, having suffered all myself,
am cursed by everyone. They say I have betrayed
my husband and have set all Greece on fire with war.
Why then do I still live? Because I heard this word
from Hermes, knowing that I never went to Troy;
that I shall live again in Sparta's famous plain
with my own husband, and be no one else's wife.
And all the time that Proteus saw the light of day,
I kept intact my marriage. But now he has gone
into the darkness of the earth, the dead king's son
pursues me for his wife. But I hold fast to my
old husband. Suppliant I cling here to this tomb
of Proteus, that he may preserve me to the end
chaste for my man, so, though my name in Greece is bad,
at least my body here may have no stain of shame.

[*Enter Teucer, a Greek hero from the Trojan war and
     brother of Ajax. He had been exiled from his native
     island of Salamis and is now on his way to Cyprus.
     He has landed in Egypt in order to consult Theonoe
     about his voyage.*]

**TEUCER**

Who is the ruler of this strong and mighty place?
It is a house that seems the house of Wealth itself,
so royal a circuit, and such towering battlements.

[*He sees Helen by the tomb.*]

Ah!
You gods, what's this I see? I see the hateful shape
and murderous image of the woman who has ruined me
and all the Greeks. I pray the gods may spit you out,
so much you look like Helen. And if I were not
on foreign soil, I'd kill you with this certain shaft
and pay you out for looking like the child of Zeus.

**HELEN**

Poor man, whoever you may be, why do you turn
away from me, and hate me for what came from her?

**TEUCER**

True, it was wrong of me to lose my temper so,
Remember that all Greece detests the child of Zeus,
and pardon me, my lady, for the words I used.

**HELEN**

What is your name and from what country have you come?

**TEUCER**

Lady, I am a Greek, one of those wretched Greeks.

**HELEN**

It is no wonder, then, if you hate Helen so.
But who are you? Where from? What is your father's
name?

**TEUCER**

My name is Teucer and my father is Telamon.
My native land which nourished me is Salamis.

**HELEN**

Then why do you come here to the fields of the Nile?

**TEUCER**

I was driven out in exile from my native land.

**HELEN**

I pity you. Who was it then that drove you out?

133

TEUCER

My father Telamon, who should have loved me most.

HELEN

And why? There must have been some reason for his act.

TEUCER

It was my brother's death in Troy that ruined me.

HELEN

How did he die? Not murdered, surely, by your hands?

TEUCER

No, Ajax killed himself and fell on his own sword.

HELEN

He must have gone mad. No sane man could do such a
thing.

TEUCER

You have heard perhaps of Achilles, the son of Peleus?

HELEN

Yes, he was one of Helen's wooers once, they say.

TEUCER

After he died his friends contested for his arms.

HELEN

How did it come about that this did Ajax harm?

TEUCER

Another won the arms and Ajax killed himself.

HELEN

And now it is you who suffer for these pains of his?

TEUCER

I do, and must, because I did not die with him.

HELEN

You went then to the famous town of Ilium?

TEUCER

Yes, helped destroy it, and destroyed myself as well.

HELEN

So Troy is set on fire, and burnt down to the ground?

TEUCER

Hardly a trace is left of where the walls once stood.

**HELEN**

O wretched Helen, for your sake the Trojans died!

**TEUCER**

And wretched Greeks as well! Oh, she has done great harm.

**HELEN**

And how long is it since the city was laid waste?

**TEUCER**

Seven revolving years have brought their harvest in.

**HELEN**

How long before that time did you remain in Troy?

**TEUCER**

O there were many moons that passed to make ten years.

**HELEN**

And the Spartan lady? Tell me, did you capture her?

**TEUCER**

Yes. Menelaus dragged her with him by her hair.

**HELEN**

You saw the poor thing yourself? Or did you hear all this?

**TEUCER**

Saw her with my own eyes, as clear as I see you.

**HELEN**

Not something that, by heaven's will, you thought you saw?

**TEUCER**

Speak of some other subject. That's enough of her.

**HELEN**

You are so certain, then, of what you thought you saw?

**TEUCER**

With my own eyes I saw her, as I see you now.

**HELEN**

Are Menelaus and his wife already home?

**TEUCER**

No, not in Argos nor besides Eurotas' streams.

135

#### HELEN

Alas! your story's sad, and sad for me to hear.

#### TEUCER

Yes, he has disappeared, they say, and his wife too.

#### HELEN

But did not all the Greeks together sail back home?

#### TEUCER

They started, but a storm gave each a different course.

#### HELEN

When did it strike them? On what ridges of salt waves?

#### TEUCER

Where they were half-way over the Aegean sea.

#### HELEN

No one since then has heard of Menelaus safe?

#### TEUCER

No, no-one. And in Greece they say that he is dead.

#### HELEN [aside]

O, I am lost! [To Teucer] Is Thestias' daughter still alive?

#### TEUCER

Leda, you mean? Dead. Yes, she is dead and gone.

#### HELEN

Oh, could it be she died because of Helen's shame?

#### TEUCER

They say so,—with a noose about her noble neck.

#### HELEN

And are the sons of Tyndarus alive or not?

#### TEUCER

Alive and not alive. There are two stories here.

#### HELEN

Which is most likely? [aside] Oh, the pain that I go
through!

#### TEUCER

The brothers are made gods, they say, and turned to stars.

**HELEN**

Good news indeed! What does the other story say?

**TEUCER**

That for their sister's sake they stabbed themselves and
  died.
Enough of this. I do not want to weep again.
The reason why I came here to this royal house
was my wish to see the prophetess Theonoe.
Will you help me in this, that I may learn from her
where most propitiously to steer my flying ship
towards sea-surrounded Cyprus, where Apollo said
I was to settle down and call my city's name
Salamis, in memory of my old island home.

**HELEN**

My friend, you cannot miss the way. But as for you,
I tell you to escape from here before the son
of Proteus sees you. He is ruler here, and now
is far away, hunting the wild beasts with his hounds.
He puts to death all Greeks whom he can seize upon.
As for his reasons, do not seek to find them out,
nor will I tell you, since it could not do you good.

**TEUCER**

I thank you, lady, for your words, and pray the gods
will properly reward you for your good advice.
Your body looks like Helen's, but your mind is not
at all the same. It differs very much from hers.
Down with her! May she never reach Eurotas' streams!
But for you, lady, may you always have good luck.

[*Exit Teucer.*]

**HELEN**

O now in my heavy pain as I build
the strain of a heavy lament,
what are the groans I must heave! How shall I call to the
  Muse?
With tears, or with dirges or cryings of grief? Alas!

Siren maidens, wearing wings,
virgin daughters of the Earth,
O come and help me in my lamentation!

137

Come with Libyan lotus flute,
with pipe and lyre to join your tears'
to my bewailing woes!
Sorrow to sorrow, grief to grief,
I wish Persephone would send
mourners to join in the dirge,
the dirge of blood, and then in her night-black halls
she would take in return my songs and my tears
for the dead and the lost.

> [Enter the Chorus. It is a chorus of Greek women
> who have been made captive and are slaves in
> the royal house of Egypt.]

CHORUS

By the blue and shining lake
where the grasses trail, I hung
my purple robes in golden rays of sunlight,
spreading them upon the shoots
of bulrushes: and then I heard
a sad and piteous cry.
Tragic it seemed to me, sad as when
a Naiad nymph with wailing voice
groans and cries out aloud
and lets her fugitive shriek ring out in the hills,
and in rocky hollows she struggles and yells
at the outrage of Pan.

HELEN

Alas! Alas!
Girls of Greece, whom foreign oars
carried overseas, a man,
a sailor of the Greeks, has come,
has come and added tears and tears to mine.
Troy is ruined, Troy is left
to the consuming fire,
because of me, the murderess,
and my destructive name.
Leda too has sought her death
and hung herself in horror at my shame.
While my husband, wandering
on the sea, is dead and gone.
Then the glory of their land,

138

Castor and his twin, my brothers,
have gone, gone too, and left behind
the plains that rang beneath their horses' hooves,
reedy Eurotas' wrestling grounds,
and exercise of youth.

CHORUS

Alas! Alas!
O what fate is yours, what god
bringing, lady, pain on you!
It was a life and not a life
That came when Zeus, who flashes from the sky,
shaped like swan and snowy-white
begat you on your mother.
Is there a sorrow or a pain
that you have not endured?
Your mother dead, the twins of Zeus,
though dear to him, have not found happiness.
You cannot see your native land,
and through her cities rumour says
that you, my lady, gave your love
to foreigners. And, as for him,
your husband, in the salt of the waves
he has left his life behind, and now no more
will you make glad your father's house
and Sparta's brazen temple.

HELEN

Alas, Alas, which one of the Phrygians was it,
or who from the land of Greece
that felled a pine to be the source of tears
for Ilium? The son of Priam took
the wood, and wrought the deadly ship
and came with his foreign oars
to my home in pursuit of my beauty,
my luckless beauty, to win my love.
And with him was Cypris, the treacherous, murderous,
bringing death to the Greeks.
Oh, I weep for my fate!
But Hera from the golden throne,
the holy bed-fellow of Zeus
sent down to me the rapid son of Maia.

139

I was picking roses then,
filling my arms with new grown flowers,
to take them with me to the brazen temple.
Hermes found me, snatched me up
through the air and brought me here
into this unhappy land,
making me the cause of war,
war for Greece and war for Priam's sons.
And by the streams of Simois
my name was there, but empty what they said of me.

CHORUS

Sorrows you have, I know. Yet it is best to bear
as lightly as we can the certain pains of life.

HELEN

Dear women, to what fate have I been tied and bound?
And did my mother bear me as some kind of monster?
For certainly no Greek or foreign woman yet
travailed with the white circle of an egg for birds,
as Leda bore me, so they say, from Zeus.
Monstrous my life has been and what has happened to me,
by Hera's fault and by my beauty's fault as well.
I wish that, like a painter, I could have wiped out
my beauty from my face and had an uglier one;
and then the Greeks would have forgotten those bad
        things
they think of me, and they would bear in mind the good,
just as they now remember only what is bad.
When a man looks for one thing only, and the gods
take that thing from him, it is hard, but bearable.
On me, however, many things have come at once.
First, I have lost my name, though I have done no wrong;
and it is worse than suffering what one deserves
if one must suffer for the things one never did.
And then the gods have taken me from my own land
and set me among foreign manners, far from friends,
where I live like a slave, whose people all were free.
For in these countries all are slaves except for one.
And that one anchor to which all my fate was tied,—
that my husband would return one day and set me free—
now he is dead, now he no longer is at all.

140

My mother's dead; and it was I who murdered her,
not guilty, certainly, and yet the guilt is mine.
And then my daughter, who was once my house's pride
and mine, grows old in maidenhood, without a man.
As for my brothers who were called 'the sons of Zeus,'
those two exist no more. My fate all ways is bad;
what kills me are my sufferings, not what I did.
And now this final blow,—that, if I reached my home,
I should be put in prison. They would think that I
was the Trojan Helen travelling with Menelaus.
For if my husband lived, I could have shown him things
known only to us two and so be recognised;
that is now impossible, and he will never come.
Why then do I still live? What fate remains for me?
Should I choose marriage to escape from my distress,
live with a foreign husband and sit down before
a wealthy table? No, for when a woman has
a hated husband, she will hate her body too.
It would be best to die. But not to die in shame.
To hang oneself and swing is an ugly death
and held dishonourable even among slaves;
there's something fine and noble in a dagger's blow;
a little thing is the moment of release from life,—
for I have come to such a depth of suffering.
Beauty has given other women happy lives,
but it is just this beauty that has ruined me.

CHORUS
Helen, that man who came, whoever he may be,—
you must not think that everything he said was true.

HELEN
Clearly enough he told me of my husband's death.

CHORUS
Yet much of what is said by people is not true.

HELEN
Much also of what they say is true and clear enough.

CHORUS
But you incline to sorrow rather than to joy.

HELEN
Because fear holds me in his grip and drags me on.

**CHORUS**

What kindness can you count upon within this house?

**HELEN**

All are my friends except the one who seeks my love.

**CHORUS**

This is what you must do. Leave the tomb where you
    sit. . . .

**HELEN**

What are you saying? What is this advice you give?

**CHORUS**

Enter the house and go to her who knows all things,
Theonoe, daughter of the Nereid sea nymph;
ask her about your husband, whether he still lives
or whether he has left the light. Informed by her,
you can be sad or happy as the facts dictate.
For now what good is it for you to grieve
without clear knowledge of these things. Take my advice,
and leave this tomb and go in to consult the maid
from whom you will learn everything. For, since you have
one here to tell you all the truth, why look elsewhere?
I too would like to go with you inside the house
¡and listen with you to the maiden's holy words;
for women ought to give each other helping hands.

**HELEN**

My friends, I take your advice,
Let us go, let us go to the house
and learn within the palace
the story of my fate.


**CHORUS**

You call me and I'm glad to come.

**HELEN**

O sad this day for me!
Poor me, what is the tale of tears
that I must listen to!

**CHORUS**

Do not anticipate your grief,
dear lady, do not cry before you know.

142

**HELEN**

What has become of my husband?
Does he still look on the light,
the chariot of the sun
and pathways of the stars?
Or has he everlasting rest
among the dead below?

**CHORUS**

Be the fortune what it may,
you must always hope for what is best.

**HELEN**

O fresh Eurotas with your rippling reeds,
on you I call, your name is on my lips,
O was it true this story that my man
is dead? O why so wildly must I speak?
I shall take it, the murderous hanging,
the noose round the throat,
or shall stab with a blow of the sword
and the streams of blood from the neck,
and force the cold steel in my flesh,
and so shall offer up my life to those
three goddesses and to the son of Priam
who dwelt in Ida's hollows with the herds.

**CHORUS**

I pray that the evil may turn elsewhere,
and that good luck may be yours.

**HELEN**

O unhappy Troy, destroyed
by deeds that should not have been done!
How have you suffered! The gifts
of Cypris to me have brought forth blood,
have brought forth tears, sorrow on sorrow,
weeping on weeping and pain upon pain.
Mothers have lost their children,
maidens have cut from their heads
their tresses in mourning for brothers,
dead men in the Phrygian stream
of Scamander. And Greece has let loose
a cry and a wailing for death.

Hands are laid to the head;
finger nails tear the delicate skin of the cheek
which is wet from the flowing of blood.
O happy once as a maiden, Callisto, in Arcady, you
who treading on four feet suffered the wedding of Zeus,
more happy by far was your lot than the lot of my mother,
you in the shape of the shaggy limbed beasts,
with violent glare of a lioness's eye,
have put off the burden of sorrow.
Happy was she too whom Artemis drove from the dance,
the Titanian daughter of Merops, and made her a stag
    with gold horns,
because of her beauty. My beauty and charm have been
    only
destructive, destructive to Troy and the dead of the Greeks.

[*Helen and the Chorus go into the palace. Enter
Menelaus, who has been shipwrecked off the
coast of Egypt.*]

### MENELAUS

O Pelops, you who once at Pisa won the prize
from Oenomaus in the four-horse chariot race,
I wish that at the time your body was served up
before the gods, you then and there had left your life,
and never had become the father of my sire
Atreus, who wedded Aerope and from her had
Agamemnon and me, Menelaus, a famous pair.
It was, I think, the greatest force on earth I led
[and here I do not boast] across the sea to Troy;
nor was it by compulsion that I ruled my troops;
no, it was freely that the youth of Greece obeyed.
Of these some must be thought of as no more alive,
and others, happily escaping from the sea,
bring home again the names of men considered dead.
But as for me, over the sea swell of green salt
I have wandered wretched every moment since I sacked
the towers of Troy, and though I long to reach my home,
heaven does not hold me worthy to succeed in this.
To every desolate and friendless landing place
in Libya I have sailed, and when I near my land
then once again storms drive me back, and never yet

have fair winds struck upon my sail to bring me home.
Now wretched and shipwrecked and having lost my
  friends,
I am thrown up on this land. My ship on rocks
is shattered into many bits of floating wreck.
The keel was torn away from the well-jointed frame;
on it by unexpected chance I got to shore
safely, and Helen with me whom I dragged from Troy.
What is this country's name and who its people are
I do not know. I was ashamed to join the crowd
and question people, and I hid my wretched state
in shame at my misfortune. When a noble man
does badly, then through very strangeness of it all
his fall is worse than that of one long used to ill.
Want wears me out; for neither have I any food
nor clothing for my body, as may well be seen
by these rags, rescued from the sea, in which I'm dressed.
The robes I had before and brightly coloured clothes,
all finery the sea has taken. I have hid
in hollows of a cave the woman who has been
the cause of all my troubles, and have told my friends,
—those who survive—to guard my wife while I came here.
I have come alone, trying to find some help for those
I left behind, if I can find it anywhere.
Seeing this palace circled with its battlements
and mighty gates belonging to some wealthy man,
I have approached it. From a great house there is hope
of help for sailors. As for those who have no bread,
they could not help one even if they wanted to.

> [*Menelaus approaches the palace door and
> knocks.*]

Is there some porter here who'll come outside the house
and then report my sufferings to those indoors?

> [*The gates are half opened by an old woman,
> who leers out and addresses Menelaus angrily.*]

### OLD WOMAN
Who's there? Be off at once and leave this house alone!
It is no good standing here before these courtyard gates
troubling your betters. Otherwise you will be killed,
being a Greek. No Greeks have any business here.

#### MENELAUS

Good woman, softly, softly! What you say is good.
I will obey you, yes; but do not speak so loud.

#### OLD WOMAN

Be off! For, stranger, this is what my duty is:
not to let any Greek at all approach this house.

#### MENELAUS

Ah, do not lay your hand on me and force me out!

#### OLD WOMAN

Because you won't obey me. It is all your fault.

#### MENELAUS

But go inside the house and tell your masters of me.

#### OLD WOMAN

Yes, and a bitter story that would be for them.

#### MENELAUS

I am shipwrecked and a stranger. No one harms such
men.

#### OLD WOMAN

Now go off to some other house instead of this.

#### MENELAUS

No, I must come inside. And you, do what I ask.

#### OLD WOMAN

You are a nuisance here, and soon will be thrown out.

#### MENELAUS

Ah! Where are now those famous forces that I led?

#### OLD WOMAN

You may be a great man abroad, but not so here.

#### MENELAUS

O God, have I deserved thus to be brought to book?

#### OLD WOMAN

Why wet your eyes with tears, since no one pities you?

#### MENELAUS

It is the happy fortune that I used to have.

#### OLD WOMAN

Then go away and do your weeping with your friends.

**MENELAUS**

What is this country and whose is this royal house?

**OLD WOMAN**

It is the house of Proteus. Egypt is the land.

**MENELAUS**

Egypt! Poor wretch, to what a place then have I sailed!

**OLD WOMAN**

What fault have you to find with the bright land of Nile?

**MENELAUS**

No fault with that. It is my fate that I lament.

**OLD WOMAN**

Many are wretched. You are not the only one.

**MENELAUS**

Is he now in the house, the man you call your king?

**OLD WOMAN**

There is his tomb. It is his son who rules the land.

**MENELAUS**

And where is he? Is he away or in the house?

**OLD WOMAN**

He is not in. And savagely he hates the Greeks.

**MENELAUS**

What is his reason? Why has this affected me?

**OLD WOMAN**

Helen, the child of Zeus, is staying in this house.

**MENELAUS**

What? What is this you say? Tell it me once again.

**OLD WOMAN**

Tyndarus' daughter, she who lived in Sparta once.

**MENELAUS**

Where did she come from? [*aside*] What is the meaning of
all this?

**OLD WOMAN**

From Lacedaemon's country she came to this land.

**MENELAUS**

When? [*aside*] My wife cannot have stolen from the cave.

Stranger, it was before the Greeks set out for Troy.
But leave this house. For things are going on inside
because of which this royal palace is disturbed.
And you have come at the wrong time, for if the king
finds you, the only gift you'll have from him is death.
Myself, I am friendly to the Greeks, although the words
I spoke were harsh ones out of terror for my king.

[*Exit.*]

MENELAUS

What am I now to think or say? I hear of more
misfortunes all about me after those before.
I come here with the wife I took away from Troy,
bringing her with me; she is safe within the cave;
and now some other woman having the same name
as that of my own wife is living in this house.
Then that old woman said she was the child of Zeus.
Can there be some man by the banks of Nile who bears
the name of Zeus? There's only one Zeus in the sky.
And Sparta? Is there a Sparta anywhere on earth
except where through the reeds Eurotas' waters flow?
Then too one man alone is known as Tyndarus.
Is there another land called 'Lacedaemon' too?
Another Troy? I cannot tell what I should think.
In the wide world it seems that there are many men
who have the same names; cities too are named alike,
and women also. There's no reason for surprise.
Nor shall I run because the servant threatened me.
There cannot be a man so barbarous in mind
as to refuse me food once he has heard my name.
Troy's burning is a famous act. I, Menelaus,
who lit the fire am not unknown throughout the earth.
I shall await the ruler of this house. I have
two things to watch for. If he is a cruel man,
then I shall hide myself and go back to the wreck;
but if he shows me any kindness, then I'll beg
for what I need to help me in my present state.
This is the final blow in all my wretchedness
that I, who am a king, should have to beg my bread
from other monarchs. But necessity compels.

It is not my saying, but it is a weighty one,
that nothing has more strength than hard necessity.

[*The Chorus return to the stage and Menelaus
retires.*]

CHORUS

I have heard the prophetic maiden
speak clear in the house of the king:
Not yet, she says, has Menelaus gone
to the visible darkness of hell, hid under the earth;
but still on the swell of the sea
he wears himself out. Not yet
may he touch the harbours of his native land;
but wanders, homeless and sad,
friendless, alighting on every coast
since his oars dipped into the sea
on the journey from Troy.

[*Enter Helen.*]

HELEN

Again I come to take my place here at this tomb.
From Theonoe I have heard most welcome words,
who knows the truth of all things. Still alive, she says,
my husband is and looks upon the light of day,
though he has wandered, sailing over countless straits,
hither and thither driven, harassed by his toil;
yet, when his labours reach their end, he will arrive.
One thing she did not say,—that he would arrive safe;
and I held back from asking clearly about this,
I was so pleased I heard he was alive at all.
And then she said that he was somewhere near this land,
shipwrecked and thrown ashore with only a few friends.
Oh when, when will you come? I long for you to come.

[*Menelaus comes forward from the back of the
stage. Helen is frightened, imagining him to be
one of Theoclymenus's men who has come to
seize her by force.*]

Ah, Who is this? Surely I cannot be surprised
in an ambush set for me by Proteus' wicked son?
I must run like a race horse or like a bacchanal
and reach the monument. This man is, by his looks,
a savage creature who is bent on seizing me.

149

#### MENELAUS

You, there, who hurry on so fast and strain to reach
the tomb's foundation and the pillars where fire burns,
stop, do not run away! Oh, now I see you clear,
you fill me with amazement, make me lose my speech.

[*He seizes hold of her hand.*]

#### HELEN

Women, this is an outrage. I am being kept
back from the tomb by this man who has taken me
to give me to the king whose wife I would not be.

#### MENELAUS

I am no thief or minister of wicked deeds.

#### HELEN

And yet the clothes you wear look villainous enough.

#### MENELAUS

Now stop your running foot and lay your fear aside.

#### HELEN [*who has now reached the tomb.*]

Yes, now I will, since I am clinging to this tomb.

#### MENELAUS

Who are you? Whose face is this that I look upon?

#### HELEN

And who are you? I have the same desire to know.

#### MENELAUS

I never in my life saw anything more like.

#### HELEN

O Gods!—for God is present when we know our friends.

#### MENELAUS

Are you a Greek, or are you a woman of this country?

#### HELEN

I am a Greek. But I want to learn your country too.

#### MENELAUS

Lady, indeed you look to me like Helen does.

#### HELEN

And you to me like Menelaus. What can I say?

MENELAUS

You name me rightly, since I am that wretched man.

HELEN

O after such a time returned to your wife's arms!

MENELAUS

My wife? What wife? Do not lay hold upon my clothes.

HELEN

The wife that Tyndarus, my father, gave to you.

MENELAUS

O Hecate, light-bearer, may this vision not do harm!

HELEN

I whom you see am not a ghost who serves that Queen.

MENELAUS

And I am one man,—not the husband of two wives.

HELEN

And of what other wife are you the husband too?

MENELAUS

One hidden in the cave and whom I brought from Troy.

HELEN

You cannot have another wife except for me.

MENELAUS

It seems my mind is sound and yet my eye diseased.

HELEN

Do you not think you see your wife when you see me?

MENELAUS

Looks are alike; but certainty prevents the thought.

HELEN

Look! What more do you want? Are you not wise enough?

MENELAUS

You are like her certainly, and that I won't deny.

HELEN

And who can teach you better than your own two eyes?

MENELAUS

They must deceive me, since I have another wife.

151

**HELEN**

I never went to Troy. Only a phantom went.

**MENELAUS**

And who is it can make such living breathing forms?

**HELEN**

She was made of pure air by the gods, the wife you have.

**MENELAUS**

And which god formed her? What you say is very strange.

**HELEN**

Hera, to take my place and stop Paris having me.

**MENELAUS**

How could you be in Troy and here at the same time?

**HELEN**

I could not; but my name could be in many lands.

**MENELAUS**

Leave me; for I was sad enough when I came here.

**HELEN**

Will you desert me, and take home your unreal wife?

**MENELAUS**

I will. Because you look like Helen, fare you well.

**HELEN**

I'm lost, finding my husband and not keeping him.

**MENELAUS**

My sufferings at Troy convince me. You do not.

**HELEN**

Alas! Alas! Who ever was more sad than I?
My dearest ones desert me. I shall never come
among the Greeks again or to my native land.

> [*Menelaus goes away from her; but before he
> leaves the stage he is met by a Messenger, one
> of his own men.*]

**MESSENGER**

At last I've found you, Menelaus. I have searched
for you and wandered all about this foreign land,

sent to you by your comrades whom you left behind.

MENELAUS

What is it? Have the natives stolen things from you?

MESSENGER

It is a miracle,—the truth more strange than words.

MENELAUS

Tell me. Your agitation shows you bring strange news.

MESSENGER

I say that you endured those countless toils in vain.

MENELAUS

These are old sorrows you lament. What news have you?

MESSENGER

Your wife has gone, ascending through the folds of air
invisible, and now is hidden in the sky,
having left the holy cave where we were watching her.
And this is what she said: 'O, wretched men of Troy,
and all Greeks, who by the plans that Hera made
died for my sake beside Scamander's banks, and thought
Paris possessed your Helen, when it was not so.
Now I, since I have stayed the time I had to stay,
having fulfilled my fate, will go back to the sky
my father. As for Tyndarus' sad daughter, she
is slandered for no reason. She is innocent.

[*He notices Helen standing by the tomb.*]

O welcome, Leda's child! So this is where you were!
And I was saying you had gone up to the sky
between the stars. I never knew you had the power
to fly. But now I shall not let you any more
mock us by saying that there is no point in all
those toils you gave your husband and his friends in Troy.

MENELAUS

So this is it. The words that he has spoken fit
true and exact with hers. O day I longed to see,
which gives you back again to hold you in my arms!

HELEN

O Menelaus, my most loved of men, the time
has lasted long, but now the joy is close at hand.
How gladly, my friends, I receive my husband again,

153

and in fond arms hold him! O long
was the light in coming, but now it is shining bright!

### MENELAUS

And I hold you. In all this time much still remains
to say, but now I do not know where to begin.

### HELEN

I am happy. The hairs on my head
seem to rise and to ruffle. My eyes
are melting in tears. O my husband, I throw
my arms round your limbs to hold my delight.

### MENELAUS

O dearest sight to see, I cease complaining,
I hold my wife, Leda and Zeus's child,
    she whose wedding they came to bless,
      the white-horsed brothers in torches' glow,
in former times, and then god took you from my house,
now drives us to better fate than the fate before.
Now evil turns to good and brings you back to me,
a husband who's waited long. O let joy be my fate!

### CHORUS

Let joy indeed be yours. I join you in that prayer
you are together, and your joys and pains the same.

### HELEN

O my friends, my friends, no more for the past
do I wail and lament.
For now I hold him again, the husband whose coming
    from Troy
I waited for year after year.

### MENELAUS

You hold me, I hold you. And countless days
I suffered till I learned what Hera did.
Yet my tears are tears of delight. In my heart
there is blessing rather than pain.

### HELEN

What can I say? What mortal ever could have hoped for
    this?
It is something I never imagined, this holding you to my
    breast.

**MENELAUS**

And I hold you, you who I thought had gone to dwell
in the city of Ida, the pitiful towers of Troy.
O tell me how it was you came to leave my house?

**HELEN**

O bitter this start of your words!
O bitter this story you seek.

**MENELAUS**

Tell me. For we can speak of all that heaven gives.

**HELEN**

O, but I loathe it, to tell such a tale.

**MENELAUS**

Yet tell me. It is sweet to hear of sorrows past.

**HELEN**

I never knew it, the love of that foreign youth,
nor the flight of his oars,
nor the flight in my heart for a love that was wrong.

**MENELAUS**

What god, then, or what fate tore you from your own
land?

**HELEN**

It was Hermes, my husband, the child of Zeus
who brought me to the Nile.

**MENELAUS**

Wonderful! And who sent him? What strange words
these are!

**HELEN**

I have wept and my eyelids are wet with my tears.
It was Zeus's wife who destroyed me.

**MENELAUS**

Hera? But why should she bring trouble on us two?

**HELEN**

Alas, my terrible fate, the baths and the springs
where the goddesses came to make bright
their beauty, and then came the judgment.

**MENELAUS**

But how should Hera from this judgment bring you harm?

**HELEN**

To take me away from Paris to whom—

**MENELAUS**

How was it? Speak.

**HELEN**

Cypris had promised to give me.

**MENELAUS**

Poor creature!

**HELEN**

Poor creature indeed! Then she brought me to Egypt.

**MENELAUS**

And gave him just an image of you, so you said.

**HELEN**

O, and your sufferings also, my mother, in your own
house!

**MENELAUS**

Of what do you speak?

**HELEN**

My mother does not exist. Because of the shame
of my marriage she tied herself in a hanging noose.

**MENELAUS**

Alas! And does Hermione, our daughter, live?

**HELEN**

O husband, unmarried and childless she weeps
for the wreck of my marriage.

**MENELAUS**

O Paris, you who ruined wholly all my house,
this has brought ruin on you too, ruin as well
on countless Greeks in their brazen arms.

**HELEN**

And me ill-starred and accursed god took away,
away from my country and city, away from you,

when I left my palace and bed,—but I never left
for a marriage of shame.

CHORUS

Yet if in future all the luck you have is good,
this will make satisfaction to you for the past.

MESSENGER

Menelaus, give me too my share in your delight.
I see it, but do not yet clearly understand.

MENELAUS

Yes, old man, you must have your share in this as well.

MESSENGER

This lady then was not our arbitress at Troy?

MENELAUS

No, she was not. But I was cheated by the gods,
and held a cloud or image in my arms.

MESSENGER

What's this?
Then did we toil in vain there simply for a cloud?

MENELAUS

It was Hera's work,—the strife of those three goddesses.

MESSENGER

And is this lady here both real and your wife?

MENELAUS

She is indeed. And here you may believe my words.

MESSENGER

O daughter, what a very subtle thing is god,
and hard to follow; for he turns all things about
easily, here and there disposing. One man toils;
another never knew toil, but is wholly lost,
with nothing certain in a fate that always runs.
You and your husband both have had your share of pain,
you for bad reputation, he in eager war.
He toiled and for his toils had nothing. Now he has
the best of fortune coming of its own accord.
So then you never shamed your aged father or
your brothers, never did what they all said you did!

157

Now I bring back to mind again your wedding day,
the torches that I carried in my four-horse team,
running alongside, while you in your chariot
a bride with Menelaus left your happy home.
For it is bad not to respect one's master's fate,
not to rejoice with him and grieve with him in pain.
I hope that I, though I was born a serving man,
may still be counted among servants who are good
in character, without indeed the name of free,
but free in mind. For this is better than to have
two ills at once,—both evil thoughts inside one's head
and also serve and be a slave to other men.

MENELAUS

Come, good old man, who often in the press of shields
have toiled and suffered hardships with me at my side,
now you shall have your share in this good luck of mine.
Go and inform our comrades who are left behind
how you have found things here and where our fortune
        stands.
Tell them to wait upon the shore and to expect
more trials for me to come, for so I think they will.
Now they must watch, and if somehow we steal away
this lady from the land, then with good luck all round
we may, if possible, escape these foreigners.

MESSENGER

It shall be done, my lord. But I have noticed how
worthless and full of lies are all phophetic things.
So there was nothing sound at all in altar flames,
nor in the cries of birds! Indeed it is absurd
even to think these creatures can do good to men.
For Kalchas never mentioned it, nor told our troops,
seeing his friends all dying for a thing of air;
nor Helenos. The city was destroyed in vain.
You'll say it was because God would not have it so.
Then why have prophets? We should sacrifice and ask
the gods for good things and let prophecies alone.
They were invented as an empty bait for greed;
and no one, without working, has got rich by signs.
Sound judgment is best prophet,—that and common sense.

[*Exit.*]

158

And my opinion too on prophets coincides
with that of the old man. For he who has the gods
for friends has in his home the best prophetic art.

**HELEN**
And now up to this present moment all is well.
But how, poor husband, you got safe away from Troy,
though there's no gain in knowing it, there is desire
in those who love to hear about their loved ones' pains.

**MENELAUS**
In this one story of one voyage you ask for much.
How should I tell the loss in the Aegean sea,
and false Euboean beacons lit by Nauplius,
of Crete, of all the Libyan cities where I went,
of Perseus' cliff? You could not have your fill of words,
and telling you my sorrows still would cause me pain,
just as I suffered then. I'd grieve for trouble twice.

**HELEN**
Yes, you are wiser then than I was when I asked.
But leave the rest and tell me just one thing. How long
have you been wandering across the salt seas' back?

**MENELAUS**
Not counting those ten years in Troy I've been aboard
a ship for seven courses of revolving years.

**HELEN**
Alas, poor man! How long a time indeed that is!
And now you're saved from there, you come to murder
here.

**MENELAUS**
What's this? What do you mean? How you destroy my
hopes!

**HELEN**
Go, and as quick as possible escape this land.
You will be killed by him who owns this palace here.

**MENELAUS**
What have I done to merit such a fate as that?

159

**HELEN**

Your unexpected coming bars his match with me.

**MENELAUS**

Has someone then desired to make my wife his own?

**HELEN**

Yes, and to heap his insults on me, which I bore.

**MENELAUS**

Someone with private power or this country's King?

**HELEN**

The son of Proteus and the ruler of this land.

**MENELAUS**

So that was what the servant meant by her dark words.

**HELEN**

To which one of these foreign houses did you come?

**MENELAUS**

To this one, and was driven like a beggar out of it.

**HELEN**

And were you begging for your bread? O wretched me!

**MENELAUS**

In fact I was, though that was not the way I spoke.

**HELEN**

So you know all, it seems, about his marrying me?

**MENELAUS**

Yes; but I do not know if you've escaped his bed.

**HELEN**

Be sure my bed is chaste and kept for you alone.

**MENELAUS**

What is the proof of this? Good news, if you speak true.

**HELEN**

You see the wretched way I stay here at this tomb?

**MENELAUS**

I see this bed of straw. Can it be yours, poor thing?

**HELEN**

Here I take sanctuary from that marriage bed.

**MENELAUS**

Is there no altar? Or is this their foreign way?

**HELEN**

This has protected me as well as temples could.

**MENELAUS**

Can I not take you home across the sea with me?

**HELEN**

A thrusting sword awaits you rather than my bed.

**MENELAUS**

Then I must be most miserable of all men.

**HELEN**

You must escape from this land. Do not feel ashamed.

**MENELAUS**

And leave you here? It was for your sake I sacked Troy.

**HELEN**

Better to flee than for my love to be your death.

**MENELAUS**

Unmanly words, unworthy of my fame in Troy!

**HELEN**

You cannot kill the king, if that is what you mean.

**MENELAUS**

Why? Has he then a body that steel cannot wound?

**HELEN**

You'll find it so. Wise men do not take hopeless risks!

**MENELAUS**

So am I meekly then to let them bind my hands?

**HELEN**

The case is hopeless. What we must have is some plan.

**MENELAUS**

Sweeter to act than without stirring to meet death.

**HELEN**

There is one hope by which alone we may be saved.

**MENELAUS**

By bribes, by daring action or by means of words?

161

**HELEN**

If only the king does not hear that you have come.

**MENELAUS**

Who will reveal it? *He* won't know what man I am.

**HELEN**

He has indoors an ally equal with the gods.

**MENELAUS**

Some voice of prophecy that's hidden in his house?

**HELEN**

No, but his sister. Theonoe she is called.

**MENELAUS**

The name's prophetic. Tell me what it is she does.

**HELEN**

She knows all, and will tell her brother you are here.

**MENELAUS**

Then I must die, since it's impossible to hide.

**HELEN**

Perhaps we might together beg her and persuade . . .

**MENELAUS**

Her to do what? What hope is this you're hinting at?

**HELEN**

Persade her not to tell her brother you are here.

**MENELAUS**

And then, if we persuaded her, we could escape.

**HELEN**

Easily, if she'd help us, but in secret no.

**MENELAUS**

That is your task. There's sympathy between your sex.

**HELEN**

You may be sure my hands will cling about her knees.

**MENELAUS**

Wait. What will happen if she won't receive our words?

**HELEN**

You will be killed, and I be made a wife by force.

162

**MENELAUS**

You would betray me. 'Force' is just a mere excuse.

**HELEN**

No, by your head I swear a solemn oath that I . . .

**MENELAUS**

What will you swear? To die, and never change your
love?

**HELEN**

Yes, and by your sword too. And I will lie by you.

**MENELAUS**

Now therefore take my hand to make this promise true.

**HELEN**

Here is my hand. When you die, I will leave this light.

**MENELAUS**

And I, if I'm bereft of you, will end my life.

**HELEN**

How should we die so as to die with honour too?

**MENELAUS**

High on this tomb I'll kill you and then kill myself.
But first I'll fight a great and mighty battle here
to keep my rights in you. Let him who wills come on;
I'll not disgrace the glory that I won in Troy,
nor go to Greece and find there all men blaming me,
I who made Thetis lose Achilles, I who saw
great Telamonian Ajax die, and Neleus' son
left childless. Then should I myself not think it right
to meet my death here for the sake of my own wife?
Of course I should. For if the gods indeed are wise,
they make the earth lie lightly in the tomb around
bodies of brave men killed in action with their foes,
but cowards they throw out on the barren reefs of earth.

**CHORUS**

O gods, at last bring happiness upon the home
of Tantalus, and let it have a respite from its ills!

[*There are sounds from inside the palace,—the
drawing back of bolts and the opening of doors.*]

163

O now I am undone! O what a fate I have!
We are finished, Menelaus. She is coming out,
prophetic Theonoe, from the house. It rings,
as bolts are drawn back. Go! And yet why should you go?
Present or absent she still knows that you've arrived
in this place. O unhappy, now I am destroyed.
Safely you came from Troy and from a foreign land,
and now you've come, you fall again on foreign swords.

[*Enter a procession of attendants with torches
and incense. Theonoe follows them.*]

### THEONOE

Go you before me, carrying the torches' gleam,
and consecrate with incense every nook of air,
that heaven's spirit may be pure for us to breathe.
And you, if anyone has trod upon our path
with unclean foot and injured it, use purging fire
and shake the flaming torch that I may pass along.
When you have paid this service of mine to the gods,
take back indoors the flame you lighted at my hearth.

[*She turns to Helen.*]

Now Helen, for my prophecies. Are they not true?
Here is your husband Menelaus in your sight.
He has lost his ships and lost that image made like you.

[*She turns to Menelaus.*]

Poor man, what troubles you have had in coming here!
You do not know if you'll get home or stay here still.
There will be strife among the gods because of you,
debate before the throne of Zeus this very day.
Hera, who in the past has always been your foe,
is now your friend and wishes you to reach your land
safely with Helen, so that Greece may know the gift
of Cypris, Paris's marriage, was a false embrace.
But Cypris wants to stop you from arriving home,
lest she seem guilty and as having bought the prize
for beauty with an unreal gift of Helen's love.
And mine is the decision,—either [as is Cypris' will]
to tell my brother you are here and ruin you,

or else to side with Hera and to save your life,
hiding you from my brother, though it was his will
that I should tell him when you chanced to reach this
    land.

[*She pauses in reflection, then turns to one of her
attendants.*]

Let someone go and tell my brother that this man
is here, so that my own position may be safe.

[*Helen falls on her knees in front of Theonoe.*]

HELEN

O maiden, at your knee I fall a suppliant.
Unhappily I bend to you and beg your grace
both for myself and him, whom hardly and at last
I've found and now am on the point of seeing dead.
Do not inform against me to your brother that
my husband here has come back to my loving arms.
Save him, I beg it of you! Do not ever give
up to your brother your own sense of right and wrong,
earning from him a bad dishonest gratitude.
For god hates violence, and bids us all acquire
the things we have by other means than robbery.
For all the sky is common to all mortal men;
so is the earth; and from it we should fill our homes,
not hold or take by force what others ought to have.
Happy it was for me, and yet unlucky too,
that Hermes gave me to your father to preserve
here for my husband who has come to take me back.
How can he take me back if he is killed? How could
your father have restored the living to the dead?
And now consider what god wills and what your father
    too.
Would god and your dead father wish it so or not
that what belongs to others should be given back?
They would say 'yes,' I think. And you should pay more
    heed
to your good father than to a brother's wickedness.
You are a prophetess and you believe in god.
And if you now distort your father's righteousness,
taking your brother's side, though he is in the wrong,
then it is shameful that you know all heavenly things,

165

the present and the future, but not what is right.
Then think of wretched me and all the pains I have.
Save me and give us this as well to help our fate.
For there is none on earth who does not hate the name
of Helen. All through Greece they say that I betrayed
my husband, living in a golden home in Troy.
Yet, if I can reach Greece and stand on Sparta's soil,
they'll hear and see that it was by device of heaven
they perished, and that I was never false to friends;
and then they'll give me back again my honest fame;
I'll find a husband for my child whom none will wed;
I'll leave behind my bitter state of banishment
and once again enjoy the riches in my home.
If he, my husband, had been killed upon some pyre,
I'd love him with my tears, though he was far away.
Now he's alive and safe, and must I lose him so?
Oh do not do it, maiden, this I beg of you!
Do me this kindness and imitate the character
of your good father. For this is the best of praise
for children,—if one has a father who is good,
to have a character like that one's parents had.

CHORUS

It is a piteous thing, the words that you have said,
and you too deserve pity. But I long to hear
what Menelaus now will say to save his life.

MENELAUS

I cannot bear to throw myself down at your knees,
nor wet my eyes with tears, for if I was a coward,
I'd bring the greatest shame on all we did at Troy.
Yet they do say that it befits a noble man
in times of sorrow to let tears fall from his eyes.
It may be honourable; still, for my own part,
I'll not do this instead of showing myself brave.
But if it is your will to save a stranger, one
who asks, and justly asks, to have my wife again,
then give her back and save me too. If you will not,
my misery would not be something new to me.
I've often suffered; but your badness would be plain.
Now what I think is right and good for me to say,
and what will chiefly find an answer in your heart,

166

I'll say before your father's tomb, and wish him here.

*[He turns to address the tomb.]*

Old man, and dweller in this monument of stone,
give back to me, I beg it of you, my own wife
whom Zeus sent here to you to be preserved for me.
I know that, since you're dead, you cannot give her back,
but she, your daughter, when her father's spirit is
invoked, will not consent to all his ancient fame
being lost; for now it's she who is responsible.
O Hades, god of the dead, I call you too to help.
Many dead men have come to you for Helen's sake,
fallen before my sword, and you have had your wage.
Now either give them back again and make them live,
or force this maiden here to show herself as good
as her good father and to give me back my wife.

*[He turns to Theonoe.]*

But if you will take her away from me, then I
shall tell you what she left out in that speech of hers.
Maiden, be sure of this, I've bound myself by oath
that, first of all, against your brother I shall fight,
and either he or I must die. That's clear enough.
And if he will not stand against me, foot to foot,
and hunts us, suppliants at the tomb, by starving us,
then I've decided to kill her and after that
to thrust this double-edged sword down into my heart
here, on the top of this tomb, that the streams of blood
may soak down to the grave, and we two, side by side,
corpses shall lie down here upon this polished tomb,
deathless in grief for you and in your father's shame.
I say that neither shall your brother marry her
nor any other man. I shall take her with me,
and, if we can't go home, it will be to the dead.
Why this? Because, if I turned womanly and wept,
I'd seem more worthy of pity than inclined to act.
Kill me, if you decide to. You'll not kill a coward:
yet rather be persuaded by these words of mine,
so you may justly act and I receive my wife.

**CHORUS**

Maiden, you have the power to judge between these
words.

167

Decide in such a way that you may please them all.

THEONOE

I follow righteousness by nature and by choice.
I both respect myself, and could not bring a stain
upon my father's glory, nor will I perform
a service to my brother which will bring him shame.
Justice's temple is within me, strongly built
in nature. And this gift I have from Nereus
I shall attempt, O Menelaus, to preserve.
On Hera's side, since now she wants to give you help,
I'll cast my vote. And as for Cypris I must pray
her to be kind, though I have not to do with her,
and I shall try to stay a virgin all my life.
And your reproaches to my father in his tomb
are my words too. I should be doing wrong if I
failed to restore her; for if he were here alive,
he would have given her to you and you to her.
Indeed there's retribution for such things among
all men, both dead and living; and among the dead,
though there's no person, yet there is a consciousness
undying in the undying elemental stream.
But,—not to speak too long,—I shall conceal those things
that you have begged me to conceal, nor will I be
ever a helper to my brother's wickedness.
For I do good to him, although not seeming to,
if from his evil ways I make him come out pure.
But it is you yourselves must find your way to go;
and I shall stand aside from this and hold my peace.
You must begin by making prayers to the gods,—
to Cypris that she may allow you to reach home,
and then that Hera's kindness may remain the same
as now for saving both your husband and yourself.
And you, O my dead father, never shall be called
wicked instead of good, so far as in me lies.

[*Exit.*]

CHORUS

No one has ever prospered by unrighteousness.
It is in justice that all hopes of safety lie.

Menelaus, on this maiden's side we now are safe.
The next thing is for you to give me your ideas
to form a plan together that we may escape.

MENELAUS

Then listen. You have been for long inside this house,
and lived together with the servants of the King.

HELEN

What is this leading to? And have you here some hope
of doing something useful for your sake and mine?

MENELAUS

Could you persuade some one of those who have the
        charge
of four-horsed chariots to give us one of them?

HELEN

I might do so, but how could we escape that way,
ignorant of the plains and all this foreign land?

MENELAUS

True, it's impossible. Now what if I should hide
inside and with my double-edged sword kill the King?

HELEN

His sister would not let you do it. If you planned
to kill her brother she'd not hide the plan from him.

MENELAUS

Yes, but we have not even got a ship in which
we could escape. The one I had is lost at sea.

HELEN

Listen. Perhaps a woman too may have ideas.
Suppose we said that you were dead, although you live.

MENELAUS

Not a good omen. Still, if I shall gain from it,
I'm ready, though alive, to be reported dead.

HELEN

Yes, and I'd mourn your fate in front of that bad man
with dirges and with shorn hair as we women do.

MENELAUS

But how will this bring safety to the two of us?

I see nothing original in what you say.

HELEN

I shall suppose you dead at sea, and ask the King
for leave to give you funeral in a cenotaph.

MENELAUS

Suppose he gives you leave. How then without a ship
can we get safe away after this funeral?

HELEN

I'll ask him for a ship from which I shall let down
offerings for your tomb into the ocean's lap.

MENELAUS

Well said, except for one thing. If he orders you
to make the tomb on land, then this excuse won't do.

HELEN

But I shall say it's not the custom of the Greeks
to bury those who've died at sea upon the land.

MENELAUS

Yes, you have made that right. And I shall sail with you
and in the same ship help you place the offerings.

HELEN

Indeed it's most important that you should be there
with all that crew of yours escaped from the shipwreck.

MENELAUS

Yes, if I find a ship lying at anchor there,
my men will hold their swords and stand there side by
side.

HELEN

All this you must arrange. Only I pray for winds
to fill the sail, and that the ship may run on fast.

MENELAUS

It shall be so, because the gods will end my toils.
But from whom will you say you heard that I was dead?

HELEN

From you. And you must say that you alone escaped,
you were aboard with Atreus' son and saw him die.

MENELAUS

Indeed these rags I wear as clothes to cover me

will be good evidence of fortunes lost at sea.

Opportune now, though at the time the loss was hard.
Misery then may now turn out good luck for us.


MENELAUS
Now is it best for me to go indoors with you,
or shall I sit here quietly beside this tomb?

HELEN
Stay here; for if he should do any wrong to you
this monument will save you, and your own good sword.
And I shall go inside the house and cut my hair,
and put on clothes of black instead of this white dress,
and dig my nails into my cheeks to make it bleed.
For there is much at stake, and things may fall two ways:
either, if my deceit is found out, I must die,
or else I'll reach my country and will save your life.
O goddess, you who lie within the bed of Zeus,
Hera, relieve two wretched people from their pain,
we beg you, stretching out our arms up to the sky
where among all the stars' embroidery you dwell.
And you who, offering my love, took beauty's prize,
Cypris, Dione's child, do not destroy me quite.
Enough of shame already you have done to me,
by letting foreigners enjoy my name, not me.
But if you wish me to be dead, then let me die
in my own land. Why are you so insatiable
of evil, always plotting love-affairs, deceits,
treacherous schemes and potions that bring death to
    homes?
If only you were moderate,—since in other ways
you're sweetest of the gods to men. And this is true.

[*Helen goes into the palace. Menelaus remains
waiting by the tomb.*]

CHORUS
O you who settle in the leafy coverts,
your halls of harmony, let me cry to you,
singing melodious bird, sorrowful nightingale,

171

come with your thrilling music through tawny throat,
come to my help in the dirges I make,
as I sing of Helen's pitiful pains,
and the sorrowful pains of the sons of Troy
beneath the spears of the Greeks,
when over the roaring levels of sea
he came with his foreign oars,
he came bringing sorrow for Priam's sons,
Paris, accursed in his wedding,
bearing your beauty, Helen, from Sparta,
with Aphrodite to guide him.

And many Greeks beneath the spear and hurling
of stones breathed out their life and in Hades dwell.
Mourning for them their wives cut their hair, and their
    homes
widowed remain. And many too were destroyed
by the lonely sailor who lit the light
that shone on Euboea's sea-girt coast,
and hurled the Greeks on Capherian rocks
and the crags of Aegean sea,
when he showed the treacherous gleam of fire.
By harbourless cliffs, through storms
Menelaus went, and far from his home
carried the prize of the fighting
that was not a prize, but a strife for the Greeks,
a cloudy image from Hera.

Who among men, though he search to the uttermost end,
can claim to have found what is meant
by god or the absence of god or of something between?
For he sees the works of the gods
turning now here and now there,
now backwards again through a fate
beyond calculation or forethought.
You, O Helen, were born the daughter of Zeus,
for winged your father begat you in Leda's arms,
and then through Greece you were cried upon
as treacherous, faithless and wicked and godless. I know
    not
what can ever be sure among mortals.
Yet the words of the gods I have found to be true.

172

Madness it is to attempt to find virtue in war
and the blades of the spear in the fight,
so ignorantly to relieve the misfortunes of men.
For if a contest of blood
is the arbiter, then there will always
be strife in the cities of men.
It was that fate came to the homes
of Priam's land when, Helen, that strife of yours
still could have been set aright by argument.
And now there are some in Hades' power
below, and upon the walls, like the flame of the lightning,
the fire has crept, and you carry
to the sorrowful sorrows and pain upon pain.

> [*Enter Theoclymenus. He has returned from a
> hunting expedition and is followed by attendants
> leading hounds or carrying nets and other hunt-
> ing equipment. First he approaches his father's
> tomb.*]

THEOCLYMENUS

O hail, my father's tomb! Proteus, I buried you
here at the gates that I might speak to you this way.
So always, going out or entering my house,
father, I, Theoclymenus, your son greet you.

[*He turns to his attendants*]

And now, my servants, take these hunting dogs inside
my royal house and all our nets for snaring beasts.

[*The attendants go inside the palace.*]

Indeed it's often that I have reproached myself;
I ought to punish slack behaviour with death.
For even now I learn that openly a Greek
has reached this land and has escaped my men on watch,
doubtless a spy or seeking how to steal away
Helen. Well, he shall die, if but he can be caught.

> [*He observes that Helen is no longer sitting at
> the tomb.*]

Ha!
Now, as it seems, I have discovered all my plans
ruined, for she, the child of Tyndarus, has left
empty her place beside the tomb and sailed away.

173

Ho, loose the bolts, my servants, bring out from their stalls
my chariot horses and prepare the chariots,
that it may be through no neglect of mine that she,
the wife that I desire, may steal away from here.

[*He sees Helen coming towards him from the
palace, dressed in black mourning clothes.*]

No, stop! For now I see the one whom I pursue
still present in the house. She has not run away.

[*He addresses Helen.*]

Helen, why have you dressed yourself in these black
    clothes
changing from white, and why have you with stroke of
    iron
cut off the tresses from that noble head of yours?
And why with pale tears have you made your cheeks all
    wet
with weeping? Do you mourn because of some impulse
from visions in the night, or have you heard some news
from home and are distracted in your mind with grief?

HELEN

Master,—for now already I give you this name—
I'm lost, my fortunes gone, and I no more exist.

THEOCLYMENUS

What sort of trouble is it? What has taken place?

HELEN

Menelaus,—O, how can I say it?—he is dead.

THEOCLYMENUS

This does not make me happy, yet it does me good.
How do you know? Could Theonoe have told you this?

HELEN

She, and one too who was present when he was lost.

THEOCLYMENUS

So someone has arrived and told the story plain?

HELEN

Yes. [*aside*] O, and let him come as I would have him do!

THEOCLYMENUS

Who is he? Where is he? I want to know for sure.

174

**HELEN** [*pointing to Menelaus*]
Here he is, sitting cowering beside the tomb.

**THEOCLYMENUS**
Apollo, what a sight in all his filthy rags!

**HELEN**
Alas! I think my husband must look just like him.

**THEOCLYMENUS**
Where does he come from? How did he put in to land?

**HELEN**
He's Greek, and one of those who with my husband sailed.

**THEOCLYMENUS**
And how does he report that Menelaus died?

**HELEN**
Most pitifully in wet surging of the sea.

**THEOCLYMENUS**
Where, through what foreign waters was he making way?

**HELEN**
Cast up on Libya's harbourless and rocky coast.

**THEOCLYMENUS**
And how was this man, in the same boat, not destroyed?

**HELEN**
The base are sometimes luckier than noble men.

**THEOCLYMENUS**
And where then did he leave the wreck when he came
here?

**HELEN**
I hope, to perish. Yet, for Menelaus, no.

**THEOCLYMENUS**
He's perished. In what vessel did this man arrive?

**HELEN**
Some sailors met with him, he says, and rescued him.

**THEOCLYMENUS**
Where is the curse sent out to Troy instead of you?

**HELEN**

You mean the cloudy image? Vanished into air.

**THEOCLYMENUS**

Priam and land of Troy, how you were lost in vain!

**HELEN**

I too have had my share of pain with Priam's sons.

**THEOCLYMENUS**

Did he bury your husband, or just leave him there?

**HELEN**

He is not buried. O, what pains I have to bear!

**THEOCLYMENUS**

For this you cut the tresses of your yellow hair?

**HELEN**

Yes, for he still is dear to me as once he was.

**THEOCLYMENUS**

It seems your tears for this event are real enough.

**HELEN**

Your sister any way is not deceived with ease.

**THEOCLYMENUS**

She's not. And now, will you still live beside this tomb?

**HELEN**

Why do you mock me? Why remind me of the dead?

**THEOCLYMENUS**

You are faithful to your husband in refusing me.

**HELEN**

No longer so. You can arrange our marriage now.

**THEOCLYMENUS**

I like your answer, though you've taken time with it.

**HELEN**

This is what we must do,—we must forget the past.

**THEOCLYMENUS**

What are your terms? Kindness from me should follow
   yours.

176

**HELEN**

Let us make peace and you be reconciled to me.

**THEOCLYMENUS**

I end my quarrel with you. Let it fly away.

HELEN [*throwing herself at his feet.*]

Now, if you are my friend, I beg you by your knees. . . .

**THEOCLYMENUS**

What do you seek in stretching out these begging-hands?

**HELEN**

To bury my dead husband is the thing I want.

**THEOCLYMENUS**

How? Can the lost have tombs? Will you inter a shade?

**HELEN**

In Greece the custom is, whoever dies at sea—

**THEOCLYMENUS**

What? For in these affairs I know the Greeks are wise.

**HELEN**

With clothes and nothing more they make a funeral.

**THEOCLYMENUS**

Then do so. Raise the tomb wherever you desire.

**HELEN**

Not in that way we bury sailors who are drowned.

**THEOCLYMENUS**

How then? I do not know the customs of the Greeks.

**HELEN**

With proper offerings for the dead we put to sea.

**THEOCLYMENUS**

What then must I provide you with for the dead man?

HELEN [*pointing to Menelaus*]

He knows. I'm ignorant, since I was happy once.

THEOCLYMENUS [*turning to Menelaus*]

Stranger, it gives me joy, the news that you have brought.

**MENELAUS**

It gives no joy to me or to the man who's dead.

**THEOCLYMENUS**

In what way do you bury those who die at sea?

**MENELAUS**

That would depend on how well off the person is.

**THEOCLYMENUS**

Speak out, so far as wealth goes. It is for her sake.

**MENELAUS**

First to the dead we make a sacrifice of blood.

**THEOCLYMENUS**

What kind? Tell me. I'll do as you shall say.

**MENELAUS**

No, you decide. For what you give will be enough.

**THEOCLYMENUS**

Our native custom is to give a horse or bull.

**MENELAUS**

Better give nothing than not give a worthy gift.

**THEOCLYMENUS**

There is no shortage of both these in my rich herds.

**MENELAUS**

And then a covered empty bier is carried out.

**THEOCLYMENUS**

It shall be done. What else is usual to have?

**MENELAUS**

Some weapons made of bronze, because he loved the
spear.

**THEOCLYMENUS**

Worthy of Pelops' sons will be the arms I give.

**MENELAUS**

We should have also all good food that grows on earth.

**THEOCLYMENUS**

Indeed? Then how do you lower this into the waves?

**MENELAUS**

We have to have a ship and rowers at the oars.

**THEOCLYMENUS**

And what's the distance from the land the ship must go?

**MENELAUS**

Until the foam on shore is scarcely to be seen.

**THEOCLYMENUS**

Indeed? Now why is this the custom of the Greeks?

**MENELAUS**

So that the wave may not wash back to shore the stain.

**THEOCLYMENUS**

I'll give you a Phoenician boat, one that sails fast.

**MENELAUS**

That would be good, and Menelaus would be pleased

**THEOCLYMENUS**

Can you perform these rites, without her being there?

**MENELAUS**

They must be done by mother, children or the wife.

**THEOCLYMENUS**

It is for her, then, as you say, to bury him.

**MENELAUS**

For sure good men won't rob the dead of what is due.

**THEOCLYMENUS**

She'll go. I should encourage goodness in my wife.
Now enter in and choose adornment for the dead.
Nor will I send you from this land with empty hands,
since you do this for her sake. You have brought to me
good news, and you shall have instead of these old rags
both food and clothing, so that you may come again
to your own land, since now I see you much distressed.

                *[He turns to Helen.]*

And you, poor woman, do not fret yourself away
for what's past mending. Menelaus has his fate.
Your husband's dead and will not come alive again.

**MENELAUS**

This you should do, my lady. It is right to love
your present husband and to let the others go;
for as things are this is the best thing you can do.

And if I come to Greece and land in safety there,
I'll stop that old bad fame of yours, if you will be
the kind of wife you ought to be to your own man.

It shall be so. My husband never shall find fault
in me. And you yourself will see it, being near.
But now, poor man, you must go in and have a bath,
and change your clothing. I shall make no long delays
in helping you. For you will be more glad to do
for dearest Menelaus all the proper things,
if from my hands you have the things you ought to have.

    [*Menelaus, Helen and Theoclymenus go into the
    palace.*]

CHORUS

The mountain mother and mother of gods
once sped away on running feet
through glens of the woods and falling of river waters,
through thundering waves of the sea,
in desire for her daughter lost,
the daughter of speechless name.
Bacchus' castanets cried out,
loosing their piercing note,
as the goddess went in her chariot
yoked with lions to seek the maid
who was snatched away from the dancing rings
of her virgin friends. And with feet like the storm
Artemis came with her bow; and with spear
grim-eyed Pallas Athene came.
But Zeus looked down from his heavenly throne
and ordered a different fate.

And when the mother had made an end
of wandering far in chase and toil
in search for her daughter carried away by deceit,
she passed the snow-fostering peaks
where the nymphs of Ida dwell,
and in grief she threw herself down
in snowy thickets among the rocks.
She made on the barren plains
nothing to grow in the ploughland there;

and then she withered the race of men;
for the herds she gave no fresh green food
of leafy tendrils. And life in towns
ended; no more was sacrifice made;
unburned gifts on the altars stood;
she stopped the flowing of bright well-springs
in avenging grief for her child.

And when she had ended all feasting
for gods and the race of men,
Zeus spoke to soothe the Mother's
hateful rage, and said:
'Holy Graces, come to Deo,
angry for the maiden's sake.
End her sorrow with your voices,
Muses too with dance and singing.
Cypris first then of the blessed
in her beauty took into her hands
the tight-stretched tambourine and the clashing din
of brass, and the goddess smiled;
she took the deep-toned flute
and was pleased with the echoing music.

O child, have you had in your dwelling
a fire neither just nor right,
and so have roused the Mighty
Mother's rage by not
doing honour to the goddess?
Yet there's power in the gleaming
folds of fawnskin, in the ivy
trailing green on holy fennel
wands, and in the airy whirling
dancing circles of the wooden rhomb,
the hair let loose to Bacchus, the nightlong feast
to the goddess, when down from the sky
the moonbeams fall. But you
have had trust in your beauty alone.

[*Enter Helen from the palace.*]

**HELEN**
So far as things go here, my friends, our luck is good.

181

For Proteus' daughter, helping us to steal away,
has told her brother that my husband is not here,
when questioned by him. For my sake she said that he
was dead and does not see the light upon the earth.
This too my husband has most fortunately won:
for all the armour that he was to lower into the sea
he has put on himself, has thrust his strong arm through
the shield-strap and has taken in his hand the spear,
pretending this to be his service to the dead.
And well for fighting he is fitted out with arms,
and looks like one to conquer tens of thousands of
these natives with his hand, when once we are aboard.
Then I have dressed him in new clothes instead of those
rags from the shipwreck; I have given him a bath
in water of river dew that he has lacked so long.

> [*She sees Theoclymenus approaching from the palace.*]

But now this man is coming from the house who thinks
he has my marriage waiting for him in his hands.
I must be silent. You we claim to be our friends
and bid you curb your tongues, if it may ever be
that we may save ourselves and later save you too.

> [*Enter Theoclymenus and Menelaus now fully armed. They are followed by attendants carrying offerings for the funeral.*]

#### THEOCLYMENUS
Move on in order, slaves, just as the stranger said,
with all the offerings for burial at sea.
Now Helen, if you will not take my words amiss,
be guided by me, stay here. It will be the same
for Menelaus whether you are there or not.
I fear you, lest some yearning may come over you
and make you throw yourself into the swelling sea,
maddened by thoughts of all your former husband's
        charms.
For though he is not here you mourn him much too much.

#### HELEN
O my new husband, it is necessary I
must honour my first marriage when I was a bride.

182

Indeed I love my husband and because of it
would die with him. Yet how would that do good to him,
if he is dead for me to die? Allow me then
to go myself and give my gifts to the dead man.
And may the gods bestow on you what I would wish,
and on this stranger too for all the help he gives.
And you will have in me the wife you ought to have
at home, because to Menelaus and to me
you're kind. For sure all this is tending to some fate.
Now order someone to give us a ship to take
these things away, and make your benefits complete.

THEOCLYMENUS [*to an attendant*]
Go, you, and give them one of my Sidonian ships,
a ship of fifty oars with all the rowers too.

HELEN [*pointing to Menelaus*]
He holds the funeral and should command the ship.

THEOCLYMENUS
Of course. My sailors must be under his command.

HELEN
Will you say that again, that they may be quite sure?

THEOCLYMENUS
I'll say it twice or three times if you want me to.

HELEN
I bless your kindness. [*aside*] And may my plans too be
    blessed!

THEOCLYMENUS
Now do not spoil your beauty with too many tears.

HELEN
This very day will show my gratitude to you.

THEOCLYMENUS
There's nothing in the dead,—just trouble without a point.

HELEN
I have my cares among the dead and living too.

THEOCLYMENUS
I'll be as good a man as Menelaus was.

183

**HELEN**

With you I find no fault. Good luck is all I need.

**THEOCLYMENUS**

That you will find, when once you give me your good will.

**HELEN**

To love my friends is not a thing I have to learn.

**THEOCLYMENUS**

Now shall I come with you and help you on the ship?

**HELEN**

Oh no, you must not serve with your own servants, lord.

**THEOCLYMENUS**

Then let it be. I'm not affected by Greek ways.
My house is unpolluted, for it was not here
that Menelaus breathed his last. Let someone go
to tell my chieftains to bring in their wedding gifts
into my palace. Now the whole of this great land
must ring with happy songs to celebrate the day
of mine and Helen's marriage and to feel the joy.

*[He turns to Menelaus]*

Now, stranger, go, and give into the arms of the sea
these gifts to him who was her husband once. And then
bring my wife quickly back again into this house,
so you may have a place too at my wedding-feast,
and then go home or else stay and be happy here.

*[Exit Theoclymenus. The attendants with the offerings also go.]*

**MENELAUS**

Zeus, you are called our father and a wise god too;
look down upon us and release us from our pains.
And as we drag our fortunes up this steep ascent,
lend us your hand: with just a finger's touch from you
we'll reach that place in fate where we desire to be.
It is enough the troubles we have had before.
Gods, I have called you often both to hear good things
and sad. Bad luck for ever I do not deserve;
I ought to stand upright. O do me now this one
kindness, and make me happy ever afterwards.

*[Menelaus and Helen go out.]*

184

Phoenician oars of Sidon
swift in the foam, dear life
of rowers and leader of dances
where dolphins play, and the sea
stands still in a windless calm,
and the blue-grey daughter of Ocean,
the goddess of calm, cries out:
'Shake out your sails, O sailors!
Loose them to winds of the sea!
Take in your hands your blades of pine.
Bring Helen back to the happy shores
and the harbours of Perseus' city.'

Perhaps by the swelling river
you will see the priestess maids,
or there by the temple of Pallas,
and join once again in the dance
or the revels and feasts in the night
for Hyacinth, whom Apollo
killed with the discus hurled
over the mark, and for Sparta
made it a day for the gifts
of sacrifice in memorial.
There too is your daughter, Hermione,
whose marriage torch is unlighted.

I wish we were winged in the air
where in Libya the columns of birds,
leaving the winter and rain,
press on and obey
the whistling call of their elder, their leader, who flies
over the waterless plains and the harvests of earth,
crying out in the flight.
Winged birds with necks outstretched,
companions of hurrying clouds,
go on your way past the Pleiades
and Orion's shine in the night.
Cry out the happy news
as you light on Eurotas' banks, and say:
'Menelaus has taken the city of Troy
and will come to his home again.'

O come, and let loose in the sky
the paths of your horses beneath
wheelings of brilliant stars,
you saviours of Helen,
you children of Tyndarus, dwellers in heavenly homes.
Over the green of the deep and the blue and the grey
of the surge of the waves
come, send the sailors winds
gently to bear them from Zeus.
Now put an end to your sister's shame
of a marriage with foreign men,
the shame she won because
of bearing the burden of Ida's strife,
though she never went into Ilium
or the towers that Apollo built.

    [*Enter a Messenger. At the same moment Theo-
clymenus comes from the palace.*]

MESSENGER

O King, an evil fate has fallen on your house.
and bitter news it is you now must hear from me.

THEOCLYMENUS

What is it?

MESSENGER

You must set about the wooing of
some other woman. Helen's gone away from here.

THEOCLYMENUS

And did she fly away or go by foot on earth?

MESSENGER

No, Menelaus has conveyed her from the land,
the one who came and said that he himself was dead.

THEOCLYMENUS

Strange tale indeed! But what ship was there to take her
away from this his land? It's incredible, your tale.

MESSENGER

The ship you gave the stranger. And he went aboard
with your own sailors, as you soon shall hear from me.

THEOCLYMENUS

And how? I long to know, for I had never had

186

a thought that one man's hand could be too powerful
for all those sailors in whose company you went.

When she had left behind this royal house of yours,
the child of Zeus came to the sea, and there she walked
cunningly with her dainty feet, and wailed aloud
for the husband at her side who was not dead at all.
And when we reached the covering wall of your dock-
    yards,
we dragged down to the sea a fast Sidonian ship,
a ship of fifty oars with its full complement
of rowers. Then the work was done in turns about.
Some set the mast up straight and some ran out the oars
all ready for the hand. Folded the white sails lay;
rudders were dropped and made secure with fastening
    bands.
While this was going on [indeed it was just this
they waited for] some Greeks, shipmates of Menelaus,
arrived upon the beach, all dressed in shipwreck clothes,
good-looking men, though rough and dirty to the eye.
And when he saw them there, the son of Atreus spoke
with cunning pity so that all of us could hear:
'Poor shipwrecked wretches, how did you come here at
    all?
From what Greek ship? And where was it you ran
    aground?
Will you help bury the dead son of Atreus whom,
though absent, Helen honours with an empty grave?'
And they were shedding tears like actors on a stage;
they came and brought the offerings aboard the ship
for Menelaus. As for us, we had our doubts,
and said among ourselves the numbers were too great
of passengers. Yet all the same we remained quiet,
remembering your orders. For you ruined all
by saying that the stranger should command the ship.
    Now all the other offerings we stowed aboard
lightly and easily. Only the bull refused
to set his feet down straight upon the gangway plank.
Instead he bellowed out and rolled his eyes around,
arching his shoulders, looking back along his horns,

187

and would not let us touch him. Helen's husband then
cried out: 'Come on, you men who sacked the town of
    Troy,
do it the Greek way, on your lusty shoulders raise
the body of the bull aloft, and throw it down
inside the prow,' [and as he spoke he drew his sword
ready for use] 'our sacrifice to the dead man.'
They, when the word was given, raised the body up
and carried it and set it down below the deck.
And Menelaus led the horse and stroked its neck
and forehead, guiding it to come aboard the ship.

And in the end, when everything was now on board,
Helen went down the ladder's rungs with shapely feet,
and sat among the rowing benches, and nearby
sat Menelaus whom we fancied to be dead.
The others, two by two, along the vessel's sides
to right and left sat down, and underneath their clothes,
they kept their hidden swords, and all the surge was filled
with shouting as we answered back the boatswain's call.
  Now, when we were not very far away from land
nor yet too close, the steersman of the ship called out:
'Are we to sail on further, stranger, or is this
good enough here? For you are master of the ship.'
'It's far enough for me,' he said, and took his sword
and went up to the prow to sacrifice the bull.
But, standing there, he mentioned no dead man at all,
but, as he cut the throat, he prayed: 'God of the sea,
Poseidon, and you maidens, holy Nereids,
bring me to Nauplia's shore and bring my wife as well
safe from this land!' And then the streams of blood shot out
[good omen for the stranger] right into the sea.
Now someone cried out 'There is treachery aboard!
Sail back again! Give orders, you, to put about!
Change course!' But standing up beside the slaughtered
    bull
the son of Atreus shouted out to his ship mates:
'Flower of the land of Greece, now is the time to kill
and cut down foreigners, and hurl them from the ship
into the swelling sea!' And from the other side
the boatswain to your sailors shouted his commands:

'Quick, men, snatch up the spars that lie about the deck!
Break up the benches, grasp the handles of your oars!
Make blood pour from the heads of our outlandish foes!'
All were upon their feet. But we had in our hands
only the wood about the ship, and they had swords.
Now the ship ran with blood, and from the stern there
    came
a cry from Helen: 'Where's the fame you won at Troy?
Now make these natives understand it.' In the fight
men fell and staggered up again, and on the deck
you'd see the dead lie still. Armed Menelaus watched,
and where he saw his own men being beaten back,
there he drove forward with his sword and strong right
    hand,
and made us dive out of the ship. He emptied all
the benches of your men, then stepped up to the helm
and told the steersman to set on the course for Greece.
They hoisted sail and favourable breezes came.

  And now they've gone from land. I fled the bloody death
and slid beside the anchor down into the sea.
When I was nearly finished, someone threw a rope
and took me up and set me down on shore to tell
this news to you. I say there's nothing of more use
to mortals than a wise suspension of belief.

CHORUS

I never thought that Menelaus, being here,
could so escape your notice, King, and mine as well.

THEOCLYMENUS

O alas for my misfortunes, caught in traps that women
    make!
Now my wedding's gone and over. If their ship could still
    be caught
by pursuit, I'd spare no trouble, and would quickly have
    them here.
As it is I'll take my vengeance on my sister's treachery,
she who, seeing Menelaus in my palace, did not tell.
Now she'll never cheat another man with her false proph-
    ecies.

  [*One of Theoclymenus' attendants steps forward.*]

#### ATTENDANT

O my master, whither are you going, to what deed of
  blood?

#### THEOCLYMENUS

I go whither justice calls me. Stand aside, you, from my
  path.

#### ATTENDANT

No, I'll cling here to your garments. It is evil you would do.

#### THEOCLYMENUS

Slave, will you command your master?

#### ATTENDANT

Yes, because I mean you well.

#### THEOCLYMENUS

It's not well unless you let me—

#### ATTENDANT

Never will I let you do it.

#### THEOCLYMENUS

Let me kill my wicked sister.

#### ATTENDANT

Far from wicked, she's most good.

#### THEOCLYMENUS

She's betrayed me.

#### ATTENDANT

Her betrayal's good. It made you do the right.

#### THEOCLYMENUS

Gave my wife up to another.

#### ATTENDANT

One who had more right than you.

#### THEOCLYMENUS

Who has rights in what is mine?

#### ATTENDANT

He who received her from her father's hand.

#### THEOCLYMENUS

Yes, but fortune gave her to me.

**ATTENDANT**
And fortune took the gift away.

**THEOCLYMENUS**
It's not for you to judge my actions.

**ATTENDANT**
Only if what I say is best.

**THEOCLYMENUS**
Am I King or not?

**ATTENDANT**
For doing good, but not for doing wrong.

**THEOCLYMENUS**
You, it seems, would like to die.

**ATTENDANT**
Yes. Kill me, but you never shall
kill your sister if I can stop it. Kill me rather, since it brings
best of fame to noble servants dying for their masters' sake.

[*The Dioscuri, Castor and Pollux, brothers of
Helen, appear in the air above the palace. Possibly they might be represented as riding their
white horses. In any case they are divine and
have come from heaven.*]

**DIOSCURI**
Now end the anger which unjustly bears you on,
Theoclymenus, King of this land. We summon you,
we, the Dioscuri, the two that Leda bore
with Helen too, our sister, who has fled your house.
Your rage is for a marriage that was not to be;
nor does the maiden daughter of the Nereid,
your sister Theonoe, wrong you. She respects
the will of heaven and her father's just demands.
For it was fated that up to this present time
Helen should go on living here within your house;
but now no longer so, since Troy's foundations are
all overturned and she has lent the gods her name.
For now in her own marriage she must join again
go home and live together with her husband there.
Now hold your dark sword back from your own sister's
   blood,

and learn to think that she is acting wisely here.
We would have come to save our sister long ago,
since Zeus has made us into gods; but we two were
less powerful than fate and than the other gods
who had decided that things should fall out like this.
These words I say to you. And to my sister I say this:
Sail on with your own husband. You shall have fair winds.
We, your twin brethren, shall be there to keep you safe,
and riding on the sea we shall escort you home.
And when you reach the turning point and end of life,
you shall be called a goddess, you with the Dioscuri
shall share in the libations and the feasts men make
together with us. For this is the will of Zeus.
And where the son of Maia first set you on earth,
when taking you from Sparta on his heavenly course,
stealing you away, that Paris might not marry you—
that guardian island stretched along the Attic coast
shall be named 'Helen's Island' by the men on earth
because it harboured you when stolen from your home.
And wandering Menelaus has this fate from god,
that he shall live among the islands of the blest.
For noble men are never hated by the gods,
although they suffer more than those of no account.

### THEOCLYMENUS
Children of Leda and of Zeus, I lay aside
the anger at your sister that I used to have.
And for my sister too, I could not kill her now.
Let Helen reach her home, if this is heaven's will.
Be sure that you are born blood-brothers of the one
who is the best of women and the wisest too.
Let me rejoice with you in Helen's noble mind,
a thing that in most women is not found at all.

### CHORUS
Many indeed the shapes and changes are
of heavenly beings. Many things the gods
achieve beyond our judgment. What we thought
is not confirmed, and what we thought not god
contrives. And so it happens in this story.